Margaret Fleming, editor

Teaching the Epic

National Council of Teachers of English

1111 Kenyon Road, Urbana, Illinois 61801

NCTE EDITORIAL BOARD: Richard Corbin, Charlotte S. Huck, Richard Lloyd-Jones, Roy C. O'Donnell, Owen Thomas, Robert F. Hogan, *ex officio*, Paul O'Dea, *ex officio*. STAFF EDITOR: Duncan Streeter. EDITORIAL SERVICES: Judith E. Jennings. BOOK DESIGN: David Colley.

Library of Congress Catalog Card Number: 74-84481.
NCTE Stock Number: 52058

Contents

Foreword

This book had its origin in a 1973 summer workshop at the University of Arizona entitled "Teaching Epic and Saga," a subject I had wanted to pursue for a long time. I was fortunate to find four others who shared my enthusiasm: Carolyn Dirksen, an English teacher at Lee College, Cleveland, Tennessee; Zana Easley, an English teacher at Cholla High School, Tucson, Arizona; Lois Mervyn, a teaching associate in the English Department at the University of Arizona and a doctoral student in English Education; and Edna Webb, an English teacher at Douglas High School, Douglas, Arizona. Since I had not been able to find a suitable textbook for the course, the five of us decided to develop our own materials, each concentrating on different epics or aspects of teaching the epic, then sharing our results.

When NCTE agreed to publish the collection of materials we had assembled, together with some suggested additions, only Lois Mervyn, Zana Easley, and I were in Tucson, so the work of expansion and revision was largely ours. Carolyn Dirksen was also able to send us some material. Although we worked closely together, credit for the final product can be divided in the following way.

Edna Webb contributed most of the suggested projects for studying epics. Her earlier work had taken a somewhat different direction from the rest, and later, distance and other commitments prevented her from participating further. Nevertheless, her enthusiasm contributed a great deal indirectly.

Carolyn Dirksen contributed the essay, "The Role of the Supernatural in the Epic," and the discussions of the Indian epic, the *Mahabharata,* the *Ramayana,* the *Faerie Queene,* and *Paradise Lost.*

Zana Easley contributed the discussions of *Beowulf,* the *Shah-Nameh,* the *Song of Roland,* the *Lay of Igor's Campaign,* the *Nibelungenlied,* and the *Kalevala.* She also helped me put together the reference list of art, music, and literature based on epics.

Lois Mervyn contributed the discussions of the Renaissance epic, *Orlando Furioso,* the *Lusiads, Jerusalem Delivered,* and the five examples of American "epic."

v

I wrote the introduction and the section on comparative translations with its sample linguistic analysis. I also contributed the discussions of *Gilgamesh*, the *Iliad*, the *Odyssey*, the *Aeneid*, *El Cid*, and the *Divine Comedy*. Lois, Zana, and I collaborated on the bibliography of translations and the bibliography of reference works.

I am responsible for the final revision, although my husband John helped greatly by reading and making suggestions. The task was more difficult than anticipated, since I had to try to make consistent not only the format of the book but the styles of four very different writers. I must apologize for any stylistic felicities of the original writers that may have been lost in this homogenizing process.

Margaret Fleming
University of Arizona

Introduction

It is difficult to define *epic* in terms that will cover all those epics discussed in this book and at the same time distinguish it from such closely related genres as *saga, romance,* and *chronicle.* Typically, however, an epic has most, if not all, of the following characteristics:

1. It is a long narrative poem.
2. Its hero embodies the ideals of a particular nation or culture.
3. It usually appears in the early stages of nationalistic or cultural consciousness.
4. Its subject is a struggle for something that symbolizes a value of the culture.
5. Its heroes are aided by divine or supernatural forces.
6. It is serious and written in an elevated style.

In addition, the classical epics usually employ the following conventions:

7. An invocation to the muse—poets felt the need of divine inspiration when celebrating epic themes.
8. Catalogs—long lists of warriors, ships, etc.
9. Descriptions of weapons or armor—such aspects as their physical appearance, magical powers, and previous history.
10. Address to the host—a stirring speech made by the leader to inspire his men to heroism in battle.
11. Descent into the underworld—the hero learns something he can find out in no other way; the trip may symbolize facing the fact of death.
12. Epic similes—extended comparisons of wartime incidents with more familiar domestic situations; descriptions of nature are especially common.

Many of these conventions are found in more recent epics, either because of deliberate imitation or similar poetic impulses.

Studying epics today may seem esoteric, since English and American works have for so long monopolized the literary curriculum. And recommending such study may seem strange during a decade when even the standard classics are being replaced by mini-courses in science fiction or sports writing. While these popular topics have the obvious advantages of familiarity, they have the corresponding disadvantage of being limited in scope and, if studied in isolation, would surely present a distorted picture of human experience.

But the current growth of elective English programs, which has encouraged such courses, may also allow the variety and flexibility to include older, less familiar works, such as epics. The desirability of studying other literatures has been recognized by NCTE and expressed in the following 1972 resolution:

> *Background:* It is increasingly apparent that English teachers need a wide knowledge of literary works in addition to those from English-speaking countries. Many high schools and colleges are offering electives in humanities and world literatures. High school and college students desire and need to understand other cultures. Now that numerous contemporary and older works are available in inexpensive English translations, it is possible for English teachers to aid in the interpretation and appreciation of literary forms through which men and women of different backgrounds have expressed themselves. Be it therefore
>
> *Resolved,* That the NCTE endorse the following requirement in secondary school teacher certification: that all secondary school English teachers have preparation in and significant knowledge of literature other than and in addition to those of the United States and Great Britain.

A major problem in teaching epics is simply a lack of knowledge upon which to base choices. While almost every Indo-European country has produced a national epic, few of them have been popular outside their own countries. However, the classical epics were standard works in the literary curriculum in both England and America from the Renaissance through the nineteenth century, and the *Iliad*, the *Odyssey*, and the *Aeneid* enjoyed the high repute that Shakespeare may already have lost today. Although these classical epics too were originally national epics, they have inspired a long tradition of art epics, the best known of which are the *Divine Comedy* and *Paradise Lost*. *Paradise Lost* is usually considered the last great epic; it transcends nationalism to deal with Christianity itself. The epic spirit, however, has persisted even up to the present. In Finland in the nineteenth century, Elias Lönnrot collected many ancient folktales which were combined to make the *Kalevala*. Less ancient, but similar, material has been used in several American "epics." The best known, *John Brown's Body* by Stephen Vincent Benét, deals with the Civil War.

The chart on the following pages lists the major epics recognized by scholars, with pertinent facts about them. It also lists some of the American works inspired by the epic spirit. The differences in length may be especially relevant. Contrary to popular belief, an epic is not necessarily long, although it is always heroic and written in a high style. The *Iliad* and the *Odyssey* may be too long for the attention span of many students, but such works as *El Cid* and the *Song of Roland* are short enough to be easily manageable and are of high literary quality. While none of the American epics is first rate literature, they have a great deal of historical interest.

Another problem in teaching epics is that epic conventions and techniques are often a barrier to appreciation. The *Odyssey*, if taught in the same manner as a novel, may well appear to students to be an inferior specimen of the genre—repetitious, contrived, and poorly characterized. The many different names and epithets for the gods and heroes are undoubtedly confusing and tend to obscure the narrative. Manipulation of humans by gods is apt to be unconvincing. But if students realize that the poet was composing and reciting orally for a frequently shifting audience, and that the repetitions and stock epithets were aids to memory for both poet and audience, they may have a better appreciation of his skill. Homer's dramatization of divine intervention can perhaps best be understood as primitive psychology—an attempt to explain human motivation according to the traditions of his time.

A third problem is linguistic. Most epics are in unfamiliar languages and in verse, and they inevitably lose poetic power in a translation. *Beowulf*, for example, is likely to be presented in a prose translation, perhaps only in excerpts, with a few lines reproduced in Anglo-Saxon to demonstrate how the English language has changed. Under these circumstances, it is nearly impossible for students to get any feeling for the unity of the epic or for its poetry.

The study of epics cannot be undertaken in exactly the same way as, say, the study of the novel or poetry. Without a

Chart of Epics

Title of Epic	Author	Date Written or Published	Date of Events	Hero	Language	Poetic Form	No. of Lines
Gilgamesh		c.2000 B.C.	Prehistory	Gilgamesh	Sumerian		1,300[a]
Iliad	Homer	c.850 B.C.	c.1100 B.C.	Achilles	Greek	dactylic hexameter	15,700
Odyssey	Homer	c.850 B.C.	c.1100 B.C.	Odysseus	Greek	dactylic hexameter	11,300
Mahabharata	Vyasa	c.500 B.C.—500 A.D.	c.1200 B.C.	Arjuna	Sanskrit	couplets	200,000
Ramayana	Valmiki	c.500 B.C.—200 A.D.	c.500 B.C.	Rama	Sanskrit	couplets	48,000
Aeneid	Virgil	29-19 B.C.	c.1100 B.C.	Aeneas	Latin	dactylic hexameter	10,000
Beowulf		c.725	c.515	Beowulf	Old English	half-lines, alliteration	3,200
Shah-Nameh	Firdausi	c.1000	3600 B.C.—651 A.D.	Rustem and others	Persian	couplets four-line stanzas	120,000
Song of Roland		c.1100	778	Roland	French	stanzas, assonance	4,000
El Cid		1140	1040-1099	Ruy Diaz	Spanish	stanzas, assonance	3,700
Lay of Igor's Campaign		c.1185	1185	Igor	Russian	rhythmic prose	700[b]
Nibelungenlied		c.1200	c.400	Siegfried (Kriemhild)	German	half-lines, alliteration, four-line stanzas rhyme	10,000

Work	Author	Date	Period	Hero	Language	Verse form	Lines
Divine Comedy	Dante	1321	1321	Dante	Italian	terza rima	13,500
Orlando Furioso	Ariosto	1516	c.770	Orlando	Italian	ottava rima	54,200
Lusiads	Camoens	1572	1497–1498	Vasco da Gama	Portuguese	ottava rima	11,500
Jerusalem Delivered	Tasso	1581	c.1100	Godfrey of Boulogne	Italian	ottava rima	14,600
Faerie Queene	Spenser	1596	c.1550	Prince Arthur	English	Spenserian stanza	35,200
Paradise Lost	Milton	1667	creation	Adam	English	blank verse	8,500
Kalevala	(Lönnrot)	1849	creation+	Vainamoinen and others	Finnish	trochees	22,800
Hiawatha	Longfellow	1855	pre-Columbian	Hiawatha	English	trochees	5,500
John Brown's Body	Benét	1928	1860–1865	Jack Ellyat	English	blank verse, quatrains, prose	13,000
Conquistador	MacLeish	1932	1517–1521	Bernal Diaz	English	terza rima variations	2,200
Mountain Men	Neihardt	1915–1941	1815–1890	Mike Fink Hugh Glass Jed Smith	English	iambic pentameter couplets	7,800
Paterson	Williams	1946–1958	1776–1945	Paterson (city and man)	English	stream-of-consciousness verse/prose	60,000

a As translated by Herbert Masor in *Gilgamesh: A Verse Narrative*, (New York: New American Library, 1972).
b As translated by Serge Zenkovsky in *Medieval Russia's Epics, Chronicles, and Tales*, (New York: E. P. Dutton and Co., 1963).

knowledge of the original language, students will miss much of the work's literary quality. Therefore, in choosing a translation the teacher will have to decide whether to sacrifice poetry for ease in reading by using a prose translation, or whether to reduce speed and concentrate on language and imagery by using a poetic translation. Ideally, perhaps, both should be used and the results compared, but this is rarely feasible. In a later chapter, a modified comparative approach that has some of the same advantages is suggested.

Instead of approaching the epic as one might a novel, by analyzing plot and characterization, it might be better to begin by looking at it as a product of a specific culture. Epics present us with vivid pictures of earlier societies, often with exact and concrete descriptions of clothing, weapons, and rituals. Students will easily see that these societies had values and traditions different from our own. For example, the divine control of human affairs in the classical epics may strike us as strange, but it may provoke some analysis of our own beliefs. Another interesting difference is that of the position of women. In the Germanic epics women are key figures, whereas in *El Cid,* for example, they seem to be almost pieces of property, and in the *Song of Roland* they do not figure at all. Analyzing these differences can often lead to provocative discussions.

Epics have provided the subject matter for much art, music, literature, and film. An interesting project would be to collect and compare several works in different media or genres inspired by the same epic.

In spite of the differences in literary convention and cultural tradition, epics have the same universal qualities found in all great literature. Like ourselves, their heroes experience loss and question the fate that permits suffering in the world. They seek glory and the immortality it promises. They value friendship; they desire revenge; and they can be moved to show compassion for the sufferings of others. It is at these points, where they touch our own experience, that they move us most strongly, and it is surely these portions of the epics that should be stressed, while the rest is skimmed, or even omitted. Although studying excerpts can never give the total experience of a work of literature, it may be valuable in giving at least a taste of the whole.

This collection of materials has been put together for the benefit of teachers who may wish to explore the epic with their students. We hope that it will give them some idea of the many goodly kingdoms in this realm of gold.

Margaret Fleming

The Role of the Supernatural in the Epic

Every epic, regardless of its cultural tradition, contains some common thematic strains. One of the most noticeable of these is the supernatural influence which works to assist or undo the hero. In some, the suprahuman element is the intervention of concerned or whimsical gods, while in others it is a sinister magic of undisclosed and foreboding origins. In each poem, however, the supernatural influence serves to underscore rather than overshadow the real human conflicts which make the epic great literature.

The *Iliad* is a reasonable place to begin, since it is the epic prototype of Western literature. In the nine-year history of the Trojan War nearly all the major Greek gods become involved. Athena, Hera, and Aphrodite are the most vehemently committed to the struggle between the Greeks and Trojans because of their rivalry in the divine beauty contest.

As goddess of love, Aphrodite seems inept at helping her hero. Accustomed to dealing with love, not war, she rescues Paris from certain death in his duel with Menelaos by transporting him to the bedchamber of Helen, his stolen wife. She does not help him to accomplish victory on the battlefield, nor does she give him courage or strength. Her personality is clearly reflected in the type of aid she believes Paris will value. Hers is, however, a solution which does not bring him honor among his comrades. Instead, they want to offer Helen and her wealth to the Greeks as a peace settlement, since they are weary of fighting for someone who seems to lack the spirit to fight for himself.

Athena, on the other hand, is more practical in her aid. She first appears in Book I to restrain Achilles from stabbing Agamemnon, but her future exploits are not so pacifistic. When the troops are discouraged and thinking of returning home, she assists Odysseus in turning them back to battle. Although she desires a Greek victory above everything, she is not satisfied with the peace settlement offered by the Trojans, nor can she be satisfied until Troy is sacked and burned to the ground. It is also Athena who gives Diomedes his strength and courage throughout Book V. A far different deity from

Aphrodite, she does not pamper her men with the love of women, but encourages them in their savage pursuit of the Trojans.

Hera is as vehement as Athena in the strength of her desire to see Paris punished, but her approach to divine intervention is also unique to her personality. As Queen of Heaven, she makes few appearances on the battlefield. Her role is to negotiate with Zeus, to plot strategy, and to maneuver events to her best advantage. Like Athena, she opposes the limited victory offered by Menelaos' defeat of Paris, and it is she who convinces Zeus to resume the fighting. She also obtains permission to restrain Ares, who has been engaged in bloody combat, and she grants new strength to the Greeks. Hera's most elaborate scheme in the *Iliad* is her deception of Zeus in Book XIV, and it is this scene which best demonstrates her powers at work. She sees Poseidon assisting the Greeks and, with the help of magic trappings borrowed under false pretenses from Aphrodite, she seduces her husband to divert his attention from the war so that her sea-ruler brother can be more effective. Her movements are carefully planned, and she knows the consequences of her actions before she begins, but she has a brazen confidence in her ability to handle her husband. Her approach to supernatural intervention is a tempering of the methods of Aphrodite and Athena. It is practical yet sensuous, and does not involve her directly in the fighting.

Poseidon, Apollo, Zeus, Thetis, Hephaistos, and Hermes also get into action and have varying degrees of commitment to the outcome of the war. However, the intervention of the gods cannot alter the final outcome, which has been decreed by Destiny. Troy has to be destroyed, and even Zeus must submit.

Because the gods are limited, their exploits take on the semblance of a grandiose game, and the human weaknesses demonstrated by the mortal combatants are magnified through Homer's humorous, yet respectful, treatment of the gods. Pride, the forerunner of the *hubris* of the tragic hero, is the downfall of Agamemnon when he demands the girl Briseis from Achilles, as it is of Achilles when he refuses too long to return to battle. However, the pride of the heroes is much more noble and justifiable than the corresponding pride of the gods. It is, after all, the vanity of Hera and Athena which has instigated the war and has kept it raging long after the human participants have lost their commitment. Because Thetis is insulted at having been given a mortal husband, her pride demands that her son Achilles bring her honor; therefore her involvement is intense. Aphrodite protects Paris because he chose her as most beautiful of the goddesses. In each scene involving the gods, Homer magnifies mortal weaknesses to Olympian proportions.

The intervention of the gods takes on meaning only as it illuminates the human situation. First, it places the human heroes against odds over which they have no control: Agamemnon has a dream which causes him to make a faulty decision; Paris, Agamemnon, and Aeneas are spirited away from battles; horses talk and offer advice; and the river rages around Achilles. Gods and goddesses appear in the guise of trusted friends to offer suggestions which sometimes lead to victory and sometimes to defeat, but the heroes are not informed of divine presences. This lack of control over their destiny, however, is not really any greater than any man's lack of control. The gods cannot finally determine the outcome; even Zeus weighs each day's battles in the balance and suffers the loss of his son. All—mortals and gods alike—must submit to Destiny.

It is essentially the human decisions and weaknesses that bring about the intensity and tragedy of the epic, completely apart from the role of the gods. It is Agamemnon's determination to have Briseis and to humiliate Achilles. It is Achilles' decision not to return to combat because of his injured pride, and it is also his decision to allow his friend to take his place in battle and be killed. His human grief drives him back onto the field, and his human compassion allows him to return Hector's body to King Priam. While it may be argued that the gods influence each of these events, it is still the human responses to the situations which make the story meaningful. Achilles' wounded pride is more interesting than Zeus' decision to drive the Greeks to the sea, and his sincere grief and remorse over the death of Patroclos is a far more vital element in the story than the wily plots of Hera. The *Iliad* is consummated when Achilles, in the throes of his own grief, recognizes a kindred grief in Priam, and all the pride and boasting of two men at war is forgotten in compassion. The fact that the gods have decreed that the body will be returned is irrelevant, since Homer focuses the reader's attention on the very real and very human feelings of the mortals. Therefore, in spite of the almost innumerable interventions of the gods in the *Iliad,* the real essence of the epic is man and his response to his human condition.

The role of the supernatural in the *Aeneid* is very similar to that in the *Iliad.* The gods involved are the same, now under their Latin names, and the reasons for their involvement are simply extensions of their previous motives. Juno (Hera) wants to see Aeneas fail because she detests the thought of a new Troy being founded after all her efforts to do away with the old one. Venus (Aphrodite) assists Aeneas, not only because he is a countryman of Paris and the primary survivor of her beloved Troy, but also because he is her son. The pride of both goddesses must be satisfied, but the *Aeneid,* to an even greater extent than the *Iliad,* is a story of destiny.

The purpose of the *Aeneid* was to glorify the Roman Empire of Caesar Augustus by looking back through history to its glorious founding. However, it is written from the perspective of the founders looking forward to a glorious future. The restraints of this mode make the role of Destiny obvious. Aeneas cannot be killed, side-tracked, disillusioned, or disoriented in his efforts to bring the survivors of Troy to Italy, where the seeds of Roman civilization will be sown. The intervention of Juno, Venus, and the array of other gods and goddesses from Olympus and Hades simply creates episodes which will clearly delineate the hero's devotion to his cause and willingness to make any necessary sacrifice.

Again, the human response and the human predicament are the interesting and significant elements in the story. The bond of love between Aeneas and his father, the poignant separation from his wife, his concern for his son, and his willingness to sacrifice love and power for his destiny make the epic human in its depth. The involvement of the gods is less significant, and the role of Destiny is all-important.

Approximately three hundred years after the composition of the *Iliad*, two great epics, the *Mahabharata* and the *Ramayana*, were being written in India. The vast differences in culture and cultural development make these stories quite different from their counterparts in Western literature, yet many similarities can be clearly discerned. Both the *Mahabharata* and the *Iliad* are based on wars which involved several nations, and both commemorate the courage of various heroes. In the Indian poem, as in the *Iliad*, the princes around whom the story is built are the sons of gods. Yudhishthir is the son of Virtue; Bhima of Vayu, or the wind; Arjuna of Indra, the rain god. The twins are the offspring of the Aswin twins, and Karna, their unidentified brother, is the son of Surya, the sun. These children of deities are pitted against their earth-born cousins in a struggle for possession of their father's throne and kingdom, and the battles which result from the conflict have much in common with the Trojan War. The differences, however, are perhaps more significant for this study.

Although the leading characters of the *Mahabharata* are the children of gods, their immortal parents seemingly take no personal interest in their misadventures. Their mortal cousins heap insults on them, and they are twice forced into painful exile, existing on hermits' sustenance, yet there is no intervention from the gods. Each of the five brothers is virtuous according to the standards of the epic, and each dutifully performs his sacrifices to the gods, but the religious practice is much more abstract than in the Greek epics. In Homer, there is always a feeling of the omnipresence of the Olympians: each act of reverence has in mind a definite goal, which is speedily carried out: Achilles asks his mother for help, and immediately she makes arrangements with Zeus for the battle to go against the Trojans.

In the Indian poem, the rituals are necessary simply because virtue itself is necessary. There is little personal contact between the princes and their immortal parents; their prayers and libations are abstract rituals rather than personal requests for immediate assistance. In the abridged, one-volume editions available, the only episode in which a god makes his presence known to a mortal occurs in a story told to the princes, not in an actual experience.

Very little is made of the divine lineage of the princes, and it apparently does not profit them in any way. Arjuna, the hero of the war if not of the epic, is much like Achilles and Aeneas in that he receives armor and weapons from the gods. However, this portion of the story assumes a relatively minor role in the entire scope of the epic. Although the armor and weapons are beautiful, their value seems to lie in Arjuna's ability and not in any supernatural forces embodied in them. In the Greek epics, by contrast, it is difficult to separate the abilities of the heroes from their favor with the gods. Achilles is a great warrior at least partially because of the circumstances of his birth, his near immortality, and the constant protection of his mother. Aeneas is likewise skilled in battle, but he relies heavily on help from Venus, Neptune, and Jupiter, as well as on the fact that he must be preserved for his destiny. The Indian princes are on their own to a much greater extent. They are skilled in battle through their own abilities, and what they accomplish, they accomplish by means of a personal power that comes through virtue. In the final bloody battle of the eighteen-day war, there is no intervention of the gods on either side. The only advantage held by the half-divine princes is that their cause is just and they have the power of virtue behind them.

As the Krishna cult became increasingly important in India, the role of Krishna in the epic was expanded, but even though he is a primary figure in assisting the princes, he is not a deity in the sense that the Olympians are; his is virtuous advice rather than supernatural magic. In short, the *Mahabharata* is concerned with individuals as human beings. Their connection with the earth is much more significant than their connection with the heavens, and their extra-human strength comes from discipline, reverence, and virtue, rather than from direct intervention or whimsy of the deities.

The other great Indian epic, the *Ramayana*—at least in the translation by Aubrey Menen—is much less religious than the *Mahabharata*. In fact, it seems to contend that the structure of institutionalized religion is a farce that not even the priests believe. Rama is a prince who follows all the rules. He does precisely what a prince should do in matters of etiquette, protocol, religion, and human relations; yet he is exiled and forced to wander from hermitage to hermitage seeking the meaning of life. His apparent virtue lends him no strength and no insight. It is not until he goes against everything he believes in that he is victorious, defeats his enemy, regains his stolen wife, and returns to his homeland as king. Menen believed that Valmiki, the original author of the epic, wanted to point out the ludicrousness of the formalized codes of religion and behavior in Indian life.

The discrepancy between the theme of this epic and the *Mahabharata,* both written at approximately the same time, results from a lack of agreement by translators as to what the poet actually wrote and what was later added by the Brahmins. At any rate, the only outside influence in Menen's translation of the *Ramayana* is the worldly wisdom of Valmiki, an irreverent resident of the Hermitage of the Gluttons.

Centuries later, the first English language epic, *Beowulf,* brings together the pagan and Christian traditions in an eerie blend which foreshadows the combination of religion and magic found in the medieval stories of King Arthur. Grendel, Beowulf's opponent, is a terrifying magic being who has cast a spell on weapons so that he will be impervious to the skill of the warriors. Yet even Grendel has a Judeo-Christian background. He is one of a long line of monsters descended from Cain, as a punishment for Cain's slaying of Abel. To the modern mind it seems odd that part of their curse should be special power, but to the Anglo-Saxons of the eighth century, the pagan tradition was still very much a reality, and Christianity had not been wholly separated from it.

In attacking the three monsters in the epic, Beowulf relies both on the power of magic and the power of God. Hrethel's corselet offers him the extra protection of paganism, and God gives him the strength necessary to accomplish His will—the slaying of the demons. Yet, in spite of all his extrahuman assistance, there is in Beowulf, as in Achilles, Odysseus, and Aeneas, a resignation to fate. He accepts it as destiny when his companion is killed by Grendel, and he accepts it as the predetermined course of things when he is successful. He believes it is God's will.

In modern times, the epic tradition is still alive. American epics also contain strains of divine intervention, in spite of a realism and pragmatism not known to the ancient writers. Personification in Neihardt's *Mountain Men* is reminiscent of the Greeks:

> And girlish April went ahead of them,
> The music of her trailing garment's hem
> Seemed scarce a league ahead. A little speed
> Might yet almost surprise her in the deed
> Of sorcery. . . . (Neihardt, p. 5)

Proximity to nature in these American frontiersmen evokes the same responses as it did countless centuries ago when the pagan myths were fresh explanations for the nature of things. Despite the industrial revolution, modern science, and nineteenth-century philosophy, the Mountain Men are also resigned to Destiny:

> Unwitting how unhuman Fate may scorn
> The youngling dream, For O how many a lad
> Would see the face of Danger, and go mad
> With her weird vixen beauty; aye, forget
> This girl's face, yearning upward now and wet.
> (Neihardt, p. 5)

Much of the similarity in style between American epics and classical epics is the result of a conscious effort on the part of the authors to write in the manner of Homer and Virgil. However, the desire to commemorate human heroism is still the motivation behind the creation of such poems. In the epics surveyed here, supernatural influence is a significant factor, yet it never approaches the significance of human responses to destiny, to forces beyond their control, and to the passions and drives that exist in all men, no matter how unheroic. The inclusion of religion in the poems was necessary for them to fulfill their function of transmitting the cultural heritage, but the focus on human struggle is essential in making them valuable and lasting literature.

Carolyn Dirksen

Reference

Neihardt, John G. *The Mountain Men*. Lincoln: University of Nebraska Press, 1953.

Ancient Near Eastern and Classical Epics

The oldest known epic belongs to the civilization of Mesopotamia, the region between the Tigris and Euphrates rivers, of around 2000 B.C. Texts of *Gilgamesh,* written on clay tablets, were excavated by archeologists at several ancient cities. Although the material belongs to prehistory, the story of Gilgamesh, King of Uruk, a man who loves, fights, searches, and despairs, is living and meaningful to the modern reader—and is the stuff of epics down to this day.

Homer's works, the *Iliad* and the *Odyssey,* concern a Bronze Age war on the western coast of Asia Minor. These epics were already classics to the Athenian Greeks of the fourth century B.C.; Aristotle and Plato wrote about them and were influenced by them. The events of these Trojan War stories provided material for the plots of the major Greek tragedies and are still used by modern authors. The *Iliad* and the *Odyssey* may be considered prototypes for the epics of Western literature.

Shortly before the birth of Christ, the poet Publius Vergilius Maro created a Roman epic patterned after the *Iliad* and the *Odyssey.* The civilization of Rome at that time was in many ways as sophisticated and urban as our present society, but Virgil deliberately set his epic at the time of the Trojan War to show the "noble" origins of the Roman people.

Gilgamesh

Gilgamesh does not exist as a coherent whole, but has been pieced together by scholars from fragments written on clay tablets. Probably it had a basis in oral tradition and was transcribed and extended later by a number of different persons. The verse narrative by Herbert Mason, on which this commentary is based, is a retelling arranged to have a beginning, a middle, and an end.

Though historical references have been found to a Sumerian king named Gilgamesh, this epic is more imaginative than historical. It has many mythical elements and archetypal symbols, such as the forest, the journey, and the sea of death. There is an obvious parallel between the story of Noah in *Genesis* and the flood narrative in *Gilgamesh*.

The experiences of Gilgamesh and Enkidu are common to humanity: friendship—each sees himself in the other; fear—Enkidu has terrifying dreams of the dark forest; and sorrow—Gilgamesh's overpowering grief at the loss of Enkidu comprises the major part of the epic.

> Gilgamesh wandered through the desert
> Alone as he had never been alone
> When he had craved but not known what he craved;
> The dryness now was worse than the decay. (Mason, p. 46)

Like all men, Gilgamesh questions fate and seeks for meaning in life, but the ending of the epic is, like life itself, ambiguous. Gilgamesh returns from his quest having lost the symbolic plant that was to cure his grief. He has found no answers. As all men must, he simply takes up his life again.

Summary

Gilgamesh is god and man; Enkidu is animal and man. In this epic, they become human together. Gilgamesh, King of Uruk, sleeps with all the virgins but has no real friend. Enkidu lives with animals until Gilgamesh sends a prostitute to teach him human ways. When Enkidu comes to Uruk, Gilgamesh is afraid of him. They fight, but suddenly each sees himself in the other's eyes, and they become friends.

Together they go to the Forest of Cedar to find and kill the Evil One. Enkidu knows the forest is dangerous and is afraid, but Gilgamesh encourages him. They kill the Evil One, but Enkidu is wounded. Upon their return, the goddess Ishtar offers herself as a bride to Gilgamesh, who refuses her. Angered, she has her father send the Bull of Heaven to kill him, but Enkidu kills the Bull, even though his former wound has not healed. This effort further weakens him, and he soon dies.

Gilgamesh is inconsolable. Trying to regain his friend or to understand his loss, he journeys to seek the wise man Utnapishtim, who dwells beyond the Sea of Death. In his grief and rage Gilgamesh smashes the sacred stones that could have helped him. Finally, however, a boatman ferries him across, and he is able to talk with Utnapishtim, who tells him the following story.

The gods decided to create a great flood. They told Utnapishtim to build a ship and to take inside all his family and the seed of all the animals. He did so, and the floods came. After seven days the water subsided, and Utnapishtim saw dead bodies everywhere. He could not understand or accept this until the god Ea made him and his wife like gods and took them to live alone at the end of the earth.

Gilgamesh cannot receive any comfort from this story. Utnapishtim says he has no wisdom to give him, but he orders the boatman to burn the pelts that remind Gilgamesh of his friend and to return him to the other shore. As Gilgamesh leaves, Utnapishtim tells him of a plant growing in the river that will prick him with its thorns but will give him new life. Gilgamesh finds it, plucks it, and returns to the other shore, where he stops to refresh himself in a pool, leaving the plant unguarded. While he is bathing, a serpent comes and eats the plant. Gilgamesh returns to find only the serpent's discarded skin. He goes back to Uruk, but finds no one to share his sorrow.

Margaret Fleming

The Iliad and the Odyssey

Homer's *Iliad* and *Odyssey* are undoubtedly the best-known epics in Western literature. Although the *Odyssey* is probably more often taught, many critics consider the *Iliad* a finer work of art. The *Odyssey* is perhaps more immediately appealing because of the variety of Odysseus' adventures, but its episodic structure and shifts in time and setting make its unity less obvious than that of the *Iliad,* which moves inexorably from the wrath of Achilles to the funeral of Hector.

The values held in the *Odyssey* are largely social and peaceful. Hospitality is stressed, and loyalty to home and family. Odysseus, who is continually praised for his cleverness, is never at a loss; he manipulates every situation in which he finds himself— whether it be putting out the Cyclops' eye or disguising himself to kill his wife's suitors.

The heros of the *Iliad* are men at war, not citizens at peace. Achilles is alternately petty and noble, and unlike Odysseus, he finds it hard to compromise or adjust. To him honor—that is, status—is primary; military valor is the means to this honor and status. There is an awareness throughout the *Iliad* of the inevitability of death and therefore of the necessity to do deeds that will be remembered in song.

The high point of the *Iliad* occurs when Hector's father, King Priam, comes to Achilles to beg for the body of his son. The motif of the suppliant, important throughout the epic, reaches its climax here as Achilles is moved to compassion for Priam and weeps, thinking of his own old father who will someday mourn for him. He is thus weeping for his own mortality and that of all men.

Achilles, then, shows a change in personal values, from concern for himself to concern for another—even an enemy. Paradoxically, this concern develops in a context in which individuals are ruthlessly slaughtered. Modern readers may find Homer's emphasis on violence distasteful. He describes death in battle so vividly that he seems to be glorying in it; more likely, however, he just accepts it.

In both the *Iliad* and the *Odyssey*, the gods intervene constantly in human affairs, protecting their favorites, deceiving their enemies, and often playing tricks on each other. Interestingly, when they appear to human beings, they almost always appear disguised as humans. Homer thus shows a sort of double causation. Advice appears to come from a friend or relative, but it actually comes from a god. The gods have more power than men, but they too are subject to Fate.

It is important to realize that these epics were composed and recited orally long before they were written down. This is one reason for so much repetition: it was an aid to memory for both poet and audience. Homer composed not in words, but in phrases that would fit certain metrical patterns. Thus he might use "valiant Odysseus" or "resourceful Odysseus," not because the context showed these attributes, but because the verse demanded a pattern of $-\,.\,.\,-\,.$ or $.\,-\,.\,.\,-\,.$ This convention accounts for the variety of names and epithets for the same person.

The epic simile is another poetic technique that Homer uses to compare actions of the narrative, such as battle scenes, with familiar experiences. The similes are also important in reminding us of the world of peace from which the warriors have come, for it is their hope of returning to that world that provides the war's ultimate justification. For example:

> The whole place was like some great threshing floor, when the farm-hands are winnowing and throwing up their shovelfuls into the wind: Golden Demeter divides corn and chaff, and the chaff is blown away into white heaps. So they fought. . . . (Rouse, trans., *The Iliad*, p. 67)

These similes are much more frequent in the *Iliad* than in the *Odyssey*, and their evocation of nature and domesticity provides a contrast to the violence and horror of war.

> Meanwhile the people came crowding on. They were like a great swarm of buzzing bees, which come on and on

out of a cave and hover in clusters over the flowers of
spring: here they fly, and there they fly, no end to them.
(Rouse, trans., *The Iliad,* p. 24)

The Iliad

The Greeks have been besieging Troy for nine years,
trying to win back Helen, who was abducted by the Trojan prince
Paris. A plague spreads through their camp, and the gods tell
Agamemnon, the leader of the Greeks, that in order to restore health
he must return a prize—a girl that he has captured. Agamemnon
obeys, but to compensate for his loss, he takes a girl who belongs to
Achilles, the greatest warrior among the Greeks. Achilles, insulted,
refuses to continue fighting. His defection weakens troop morale;
many of the Greeks want to return home, but eventually they are
persuaded to stay. Paris then challenges Helen's husband Menelaos
to a duel to settle the war. Menelaos accepts and they fight, but just
as Paris is about to be killed, the goddess Aphrodite snatches him
up and takes him to Helen's bedchamber. So no one is victorious
and the war goes on. The heroes on both sides, aided by their favorite
gods, fight nobly and show their valor, while Achilles sulks in his tent.
Finally Agamemnon sends envoys to him, offers to give back his girl,
and promises many valuable gifts if he will rejoin the army. Achilles
refuses.

With the help of a divine stratagem, the Trojans begin to
gain the advantage. Achilles' friend Patroclos, who had also with-
drawn from the fighting, insists on returning to the battle. Achilles
reluctantly consents to his going and lends him his own armor.
Patroclos fights nobly, but he cannot overcome the great Trojan hero
Hector. Hector kills him and strips him of the armor.

Now Achilles is infuriated and decides to fight Hector.
His goddess mother procures him new armor from the god Hephaistos, in which, and with the aid of another divine stratagem, he is able
to kill Hector. To avenge the loss of Patroclos, he drags the body three
times around the walls of Troy. When he returns triumphant, the
Greeks hold funeral games in Patroclos' honor.

Meanwhile Hector's father, King Priam of Troy, prepares
to approach Achilles and beg for the body of his son. The gods
grant him safe-conduct through the Greek lines. Achilles, moved by
the old man's grief, grants his request. Thus Hector is buried with
honor.

The Odyssey

Odysseus, one of the Greek victors of the Trojan War,
has been trying to return home for ten years but has been prevented

by the enmity of the gods. When the epic opens, he is a prisoner on the island of the nymph Calypso, who wants him to stay with her forever.

Meanwhile, at home in Ithaca, his wife Penelope is trying to put off the many suitors who, presuming Odysseus dead, want to marry her and control his estate. While waiting for her to choose one of them, they use up Odysseus' wealth—eating, drinking, and carousing.

It is now twenty years since Odysseus left home. His son Telemachus has grown to manhood. No longer able to endure the arrogance of the suitors, he determines to find his father. Accompanied by the goddess Athena in disguise, he goes to Lacedemon, where Menelaos is king. There he finds the beautiful Helen living with her husband as happily as if the Trojan War had never taken place. They welcome Telemachus and entertain him bountifully, recalling the exploits of his father in the Trojan War.

While Telemachus is feasting in Lacedemon, the gods order Calypso to let Odysseus go. She helps him build a raft, and he is carried through a storm to the land of King Alcinoos. The king's daughter Nausicaa finds him on the beach and takes him to her father. He is welcomed and, after excelling in athletic games the next day, recounts for the company the story of his wanderings since the war.

He tells how his men ate the drugged fruit in the land of the Lotus-Eaters and had to be forced back to the ships, how they went on to the land of the Cyclopes, where they were captured and several of them eaten by the cyclops Polyphemus before Odysseus blinded the monster's single eye and escaped. He recounts their adventures on the Island of the Winds and in the Land of the Midnight Sun, and their transformation into animals by the sorceress Circe. Odysseus explains that the gods rescued him from this fate but told him he had to visit the kingdom of the dead, to seek advice from the blind seer Teiresias, before he could find his way home. Odysseus then describes how, after returning from that journey, he set sail again and managed to escape the lure of the singing sirens, and the terrors of Scylla and Charybdis. In the Land of the Sun God his men killed the god's cattle and were punished by drowning. He tells how he alone survived that fate and was cast up on Calypso's island, where he stayed seven years. Now, he says, he wants only to return home.

King Alcinoos, impressed by his story, provides him with a ship, and he sails to Ithaca. There he is met by Athena, who helps him devise a stratagem to foil the suitors. While she goes off to Lacedemon to fetch Telemachus, Odysseus, disguised as an old man, visits a loyal swineherd and hears from him of the situation at the palace. He tells only Telemachus who he is before returning to his home, still in disguise. There he is recognized by his dog and his old nurse, but not by his wife.

Following Athena's advice, Penelope announces that she will marry whichever suitor can win a shooting contest using her husband's bow. Odysseus enters the contest and wins easily. He then reveals himself to the suitors and, with Telemachus' help, massacres them. Penelope is afraid to accept him until he convinces her of his identity by telling the secret of their marriage bed. Athena blesses their reunion by holding back the dawn so they can enjoy a long night together. Thus Odysseus regains his home and kingdom.

Margaret Fleming

The Aeneid

In the *Aeneid,* Virgil traces the grandeur of Rome under Augustus Caesar back to the glory of ancient Troy. Aeneas, the son of the goddess Venus, is one of the Trojans who survives the fall of Troy; after years of wandering, he reaches Italy, subdues the Latins, and becomes the ancestor of Romulus and Remus, the legendary founders of Rome. Throughout the epic Virgil keeps the future of the Roman Empire before the reader by a series of prophecies and visions.

Homer's epics were familiar to Virgil and his audience; thus Virgil gained stature for the *Aeneid* by imitating them. The *Aeneid* is linked to the *Iliad* and the *Odyssey* not only by its subject matter, but also by its style and structure. Virgil uses Homer's meter—dactylic hexameter—and the same techniques of epic simile and manipulation by the gods. The first half of the *Aeneid* recalls the *Odyssey* as it traces the wanderings of Aeneas; the second half recalls the *Iliad* in its description of the conflict between Trojans and Latins.

Like Homer, Virgil excels at vivid descriptions, such as this of Priam's death:

> Even as he spoke, he dragged the old man, trembling,
> And sliding in the pool of his son's blood, right to the altar;
> Twined Priam's hair in his left hand, raised with his right the flashing
> Sword, and sank it up to the hilt between his ribs.
> (Day-Lewis, p. 51)

Virgil's characterization, however, shows more depth than Homer's. Aeneas, for example, seems closer to us than the stylized heroes of the *Iliad.* His epithet is *pius,* not the English "pious," but something closer to "responsible." And he does assume, sometimes unwillingly, many responsibilities: for his father and son, for his band of surviving Trojans, and ultimately for the destiny of Rome. In every situation of conflict between duty and personal desire, duty wins. He loses his wife; he is refused permission to settle among friends; and he has to renounce his love for Dido—his most painful sacrifice:

> Aeneas, mindful of Jove's words, kept his eyes
> Unyielding, and with a great effort repressed his feeling
> for her.
>
> . . .
>
> "God's will, not mine, says 'Italy.' "
> (Day-Lewis, pp. 91–92)

Of special interest in the *Aeneid* are the story of the fall of Troy through the stratagem of the Trojan Horse (Book II), the description of the funeral games for Anchises (Book V), and Aeneas' visit to the underworld (Book VI). The last half of the epic is generally felt to lack the power of the first half. Since Virgil was still working on it at the time of his death, many critics believe that it would have been improved had he lived to complete it to his satisfaction.

Summary

Aeneas and a band of other Trojan survivors, guided by destiny and pursued by the hostility of the goddess Juno, arrive at Carthage. Queen Dido welcomes them and asks to hear their story. Aeneas tells of the fall of Troy.

The Greeks, he says, entered the city in the Trojan Horse and began to loot and kill. In the midst of the confusion, his mother Venus appeared to him and told him to flee, for he was destined to found a new Troy. He recounts how he left the burning city with his household gods, carrying his old father on his back and leading his little son by the hand. His wife followed for a short distance, but since she was not destined to go with him any farther, she was lost behind. Aeneas then recalls how his little band of Trojans wandered for several years, driven by Juno's hatred. Several times they attempted to found a new city, but each time a supernatural sign warned them to go on farther. Like Odysseus, they had many adventures. They touched on the land of the Cyclopes, but were warned off in time to escape the monsters. With sorrow Aeneas tells Dido how, at the last stop before Carthage, he lost his old father.

Dido is deeply moved by this tale. She falls in love with Aeneas and begs him to remain and share her kingdom. Aeneas is willing and they become lovers, but after a winter in Carthage, he receives a message from the gods reminding him that his destiny is elsewhere. Reluctantly he prepares to leave. Dido tries desperately to persuade him to stay, but his sense of duty does not waver. After he leaves, Dido kills herself.

At the next port Aeneas holds funeral games in honor of his father. He visits the shrine of the sibyl, a prophetess who tells him he must visit the underworld and gives him directions for finding the way. There he is rejected by the ghost of Dido, but he talks to many old friends. His father meets him and guides him to a vision of the glorious future of Rome—the second Troy that his descendants will found.

Inspired, Aeneas returns and sets out once more and finally arrives in Italy. There, a supernatural sign tells him that this is the place destined for his future home. He and his party are welcomed by King Latinus, who agrees to give them a piece of land on which to settle and offers his daughter Lavinia as a bride for Aeneas, for, he says, her destiny is to wed a foreigner. Another warrior, Turnus, who has been engaged to Lavinia, feels cheated and, further inflamed by Juno's hatred, prepares to do battle with the Trojans. The resulting war draws in various Italian tribes as allies on both sides. Many brave heroes are killed before Aeneas kills Turnus and wins his promised bride and his right to establish Rome.

Margaret Fleming

References

Day-Lewis, C., trans. *The Aeneid*. New York: Doubleday and Co., Anchor Books, 1952.

Mason, Herbert, trans. *Gilgamesh: A Verse Narrative*. Boston: Houghton Mifflin, 1971.

Rouse, William H. D., trans. *The Iliad*. New York: New American Library, Mentor Books, 1966.

Epics of India

Like Greece, ancient India has two great epics, the *Mahabharata* and the *Ramayana*. Both were first composed about 500 B.C. but have been expanded through the centuries to many times their original size. Indian epics have always enjoyed a popularity with the people that the prescribed codes of religion have not; therefore many generations of priests and philosophers added their thoughts to the poems to insure themselves future audiences.

The *Mahabharata* is the story of a great war that took place about 1300 B.C. Eight hundred years later the poet Vyasa compiled in writing the many tales, songs, and poems commemorating the heroes of that war. During the eight centuries of oral tradition, the historical basis of the poem had been greatly eroded, but even after it was written down the *Mahabharata* assumed no final form, many different authors adding passages of moral instruction as well as their own favorite stories of heroes. In spite of attempts between 500 and 700 A.D. to fix the length and content of the epic, it continued to grow and now contains over 90,000 couplets—seven times the length of the *Iliad* and the *Odyssey* combined.

The triumph of virtue is demonstrated in the *Mahabharata*, as its heroes overcome many trials and are eventually restored to their rightful places. The teachings of the cult of Krishna gradually came to dominate the epic, the best-known expression of these teachings being the *Bhagavad Gita*, a long devotional discourse which the god Krishna addresses to the hero Arjuna before he goes into battle. The *Bhagavad Gita* is likely to be more familiar to Western readers than the rest of the epic, for it has often been translated and published as a self-contained work.

Romesh C. Dutt (Dutta), who has translated portions of both Indian epics, says of the *Mahabharata* that it is especially impressive in the "grand simplicity of its narrative" as well as in its delineation of heroic character:

> And the helmet-wearing Arjun marked his son among his foes,

> Wheeled from far his battle-chariot and in wrath terriffic
>   rose!
> "Arjun!" "Arjun!" cried the Kurus, and in panic broke
>   and fled,
> Steed and tusker turned from battle, soldiers fell among
>   the dead. . . . (Dutt, p. 259)

In the poetic form he employs, Dutt has reproduced closely the Sanskrit *sloka*—or couplet—in which both epics are composed.

The *Ramayana,* by Valmiki, is the story of Prince Rama's banishment from his northern kingdom into the wilderness of southern India and his many adventures there. The story takes place at a time when there were two great kingdoms in northern India, Kosala and Videha, both famed for their piety and learning. Their universities attracted scholars from far away and produced such classics of Indian literature and philosophy as the *Vedic Hymns,* the *Brahmanas,* and the *Upanishads.*

In this poem the historical setting is idealized. The poet looks back to it as a remote golden age. Ayodhya, the capital of Kosala, is the beautiful seat of learning, whose king is an ideal monarch, serving his loyal people. Rama, the eldest prince, is praised for his fortitude and filial duty. And Sita, his wife, is the epitome of faithful devotion to her husband. For centuries the Indian people have looked up to these heroes as models for virtuous behavior.

Unlike the heroic and stirring *Mahabharata,* the *Ramayana* is subdued in tone. Reflection upon moral purpose, introspection, and faithful endurance are its hallmarks. And the trials portrayed in it are expressed in terms that are personal rather than national or divine. As Dutt says,

> A pious reverence for the past pervades the
> great Epic; a lofty admiration of what is true
> and ennobling in the human character sancti-
> fies the work; and delineations of the domestic
> life and the domestic virtues of the ancient
> Hindus, rich in tenderness and pathos, endear
> the picture to the hearts of the people of
> India to the present day. (Dutt, p. 155)

Both in its tone and in its subject matter, the *Ramayana* has had a great influence upon the development of Indian languages and literature.

The growth of the *Ramayana* differs from that of the *Mahabharata* in that it grew, not by incorporating additional incidents and passages, but by repeating and varying the same basic story. Portions of it thus degenerate into seemingly endless repetition.

Aubrey Menen gives his translation of the *Ramayana* a personal interpretation. He believes that the author, Valmiki, was part of a "dropout" movement among the intelligentsia during the Indian Enlightenment, a movement that also inspired the teachings of Gautama Buddha. According to Menen, when the Brahmins regained control of Indian thought after the Buddha's death, they rewrote the *Ramayana* to serve their own ends. Menen retells the story as he believes Valmiki intended it. In his interpretation the epic is not a model but a satire. Far from glorifying the state, it demonstrates the stupidity and selfishness of the ruling class and the gullibility of their subjects. Neither is it a glorification of the gods. And the hero, though well-meaning, is depicted as pedantic and naive. The only character presented as being clever is Valmiki himself.

The Mahabharata

Some fourteen centuries B.C. the king of a northern Indian nation dies, leaving five sons, all the offspring of gods, in the care of his blind brother, who succeeds him. Although the five princes are raised along with the blind king's one hundred sons, a fierce jealousy grows among the cousins. Yudhishthir, oldest of the five, is the rightful heir to the throne, but Duryodhan, oldest of the hundred, is very ambitious and wants the crown for himself. His devious tricks lead eventually to the great war which climaxes the epic.

Arjun, Yudhishthir's younger brother, is a skilled archer and receives armor and weapons from the gods. Each brother is skilled in some area, but in spite of their regal birth and divine lineage, the five princes and their mother spend much of their lives in exile. Duryodhan drives them from the palace and attempts to burn them in their small home, but they escape and disguise themselves as hermit priests. In this guise, and through Arjun's skill in archery, they win the hand of the beautiful princess Draupadi, who marries Yudhishthir. With her powerful father behind them, the brothers force Duryodhan to give them their inheritance. He divides the kingdom, giving Yudhishthir the richest portion.

After his ritualistic coronation, Yudhishthir becomes a powerful and benevolent king. He is well-loved, but has a fatal weakness—gambling. Duryodhan exploits this weakness by sending an emissary with loaded dice, who wins Yudhishthir's crown, lands, wealth, brothers, and wife Draupadi. Yudhishthir himself has to become a slave to pay his debt.

Duryodhan greatly insults Draupadi, but his father, the blind former king, grants her three wishes in an attempt to make up for his son's rudeness. She asks for the freedom of her husband and his brothers and Duryodhan grants it on condition that they go into exile.

For twelve years the five brothers and Draupadi live as hermits in the forest. During the thirteenth year they conceal themselves as servants in the household of a powerful neighboring king. On one occasion, during the king's absence, Duryodhan's soldiers raid his cattle. The prince is unable to protect his father's property, but the five brothers come to his aid and drive the soldiers out. When they reveal their identities the king, in gratitude, gives his daughter in marriage to Arjun's son.

Gathered for the wedding, the leaders and elders from neighboring kingdoms support Yudhishthir's claim to his former throne. He petitions Duryodhan to return it to him now that the specified terms of the exile have been fulfilled. Duryodhan refuses.

Both Yudhishthir and Duryodhan now enlist allies from neighboring kingdoms and prepare for a monumental war. As they are drawn up for battle, the god Krishna appears to Arjun and attempts to answer his questions about the validity of war. This is the section of the poem known as the *Bhagavad Gita*.

After eighteen days of slaughter, Yudhishthir is victorious and resumes his position as king. However, many of his friends and kinsmen, including Arjun's son, have been killed, and the victory is a hollow one.

The Ramayana

Rama, heir to the throne of the Kosalas, marries the beautiful Sita, daughter of the king of the Videhas. Although he is a faithful son, his step-mother tricks his father into banishing him for fourteen years and into making her son, Bharat, heir apparent. Rama is told of this decision as he is preparing for his coronation, but he accepts his father's will without complaining. Followed by his wife Sita and a brother, Lakshman, he goes into exile. His father soon dies of grief.

When Rama's brother Bharat, who has been absent from home, learns of his mother's trick, he is horrified and follows Rama to urge him to return. But Rama says he has promised his father to live the life of a hermit for fourteen years and will not go back until then. So Bharat places Rama's sandals on the throne and administers the kingdom as Rama's deputy.

Rama, Sita, and Lakshman wander from place to place, encountering many adventures. At one point they injure a she-demon, who inspires her brother Ravan, the King of Ceylon, to avenge her. She tricks Rama and Lakshman into leaving Sita alone in the forest, whereupon Ravan abducts her and carries her off to his palace. There she maintains her honor, refusing to submit to Ravan's propositions.

Meanwhile Rama and Lakshman wander around mourning and searching for Sita. Finally a friendly chief with magical powers discovers her in Ceylon and brings back a token to Rama. Rama gathers his allies; they make a causeway across the ocean to Ceylon and defeat Ravan in a great battle.

News of Rama's victory reaches his home, and the people send for him to come back. Sita's reputation has been tarnished because she was so long in Ravan's court, but she undergoes an ordeal by fire to prove her faithfulness to Rama, and he accepts her again as his wife. They return to Kosala, where Rama is consecrated as king.

Carolyn Dirksen

Reference

Dutt [Dutta], Romesh C., trans. *The Ramayana and Mahabharata.* London: J. M. Dent and Sons, 1972.

National Epics

The seven diverse works considered in this section may be grouped together for convenience under the heading "national epics."

Beowulf, first long poem in English literature, written about 725 by the Anglo-Saxon settlers of the British Isles about their Scandinavian forebears. The manuscript which survives dates from about the year 1000.

The Shah-Nameh, history of the kings of Persia from mythical times, completed in 1010 by Abdul Kasim Firdausi and based on earlier written materials.

The Song of Roland, French epic written about 1100 concerning a knight serving under Charlemagne.

El Cid, Spanish epic written about 1140 concerning a hero in the Spanish wars against the Moors.

The Lay of Igor's Campaign, Russian epic written sometime after 1185 concerning the efforts of the Prince of Kiev to expel the Kumans, a nomadic tribe, from southern Russia. The author was allegedly an eye-witness to the events.

The Nibelungenlied, Germanic epic written about 1200 concerning semihistorical heroes and heroines. The events described go back to the overthrow of the Burgundian kingdom at Worms by the Huns in 437.

The Kalevala, Finnish epic compiled by Elias Lönnrot in 1849 and based on folk tales, songs, and stories preserved through oral retelling.

While the epics considered in previous chapters may also be termed "national epics," and while many later works also celebrate national consciousness and national achievement, these seven seem especially deserving of the term. All reflect the development of a national, cultural, and political identity. Five of the seven, written during the Medieval period, are significant because they date from the early stages of nationalistic consciousness. The remaining two, the *Shah-*

Nameh and the *Kalevala,* were based on earlier sources, oral or written, covering a long span of history. It may be said that the Persian
and Finnish national "epics" reached their final forms in these works.

Beowulf

Beowulf, the first long poem in English literature, was written in Old English (Anglo-Saxon) some twelve hundred years ago.
Because of a fire in 1731 that partially destroyed the manuscript, the
poem comes to us with a number of words and lines missing. This
epic deals not with native Englishmen but with their ancestors, the
Danes and the Geats. The events in *Beowulf* took place sometime
after the first invasion of England by Germanic tribes.

Because of the many allusions to Christianity, it is generally assumed that the author of *Beowulf* in its present form was a
Christian. But the Geats and the Danes portrayed in this epic,
whether they were Christian or not, nevertheless retained their pagan
traditions. For example, if a murder was committed, the kinsmen
of the victim could determine a certain amount of money the slayer
must pay; this was called *wergild.* The relationship between kin, so
important to these ancient people, is exemplified in *Beowulf* when
Grendel's mother comes to Heorot to avenge her son's death. Even
the villains of this epic live by the conventions of their day.

Another value of the warrior society of *Beowulf* is loyalty
to a leader. A feeling of mutual trust existed between the king and
his followers, and he would richly reward them for deeds of loyalty
and bravery.

The funeral practices of the Geats are illustrated in the
rites for Beowulf's death. His men built a funeral pyre and after
cremation placed his ashes, along with all the riches he had won, in a
monument on a high hill overlooking the sea.

> So the Geats who had shared his hall mourned the death of
> their lord, and said that of all kings he was the gentlest
> and most gracious of men, the kindest to his people and
> the most desirous of renown. (Wright, p. 101)

Summary

Beowulf, a Geat, hears of the cruel plight of the Danish
king Hrothgar, an old and loyal friend of Beowulf's father. Hrothgar
has built a splendid mead hall called Heorot, but a horrible monster
named Grendel inhabits the place by night and kills any Danes who
try to enter it. Beowulf and his men sail to the aid of Hrothgar.

Arriving in Hrothgar's kingdom, Beowulf promises him to
rid Heorot of Grendel. That evening he and his men sleep in the

hall, and before long the monster comes. Because of a charm, Grendel cannot be harmed by any weapon, so Beowulf has to wrestle with him. He mortally wounds Grendel by tearing off his arm, and the monster drags himself away to die.

The next day the Danes celebrate the defeat of Grendel; Beowulf is given many honors, but their joy is short-lived. That evening Grendel's mother invades the hall to avenge her son's death and kills one of the Danes. As soon as Beowulf learns of it, he sets out to find Grendel's mother.

Grendel's mother has a lair at the bottom of a boiling sea. Beowulf swims down, finds her, and kills her. When he returns, after having been given up for dead, he is rewarded with many gifts. He goes home and shows his king, Hygelac, his treasures. The king gives him a position of high honor, and upon his death Beowulf becomes king of the Geats.

When Beowulf has ruled his people for fifty years, a terrible dragon threatens his kingdom. He and his men seek out the dragon, where it lies guarding a hoard of treasure, but Beowulf is mortally wounded in the fight. Wiglaf, his youngest warrior, kills the dragon, but too late to save Beowulf. The old king dies, lamented by the people, and Wiglaf takes over the kingdom.

Zana Easley

The Shah-Nameh

The *Shah-Nameh* was begun about 829 A.D. by order of the Persian King Yezdijird for the purpose of preserving information he had collected about his predecessors. It was continued by Abdul Kasim Firdausi, born about 950, whose skill as a poet came to the notice of King Mahmud. The king commissioned him to complete the *Shah-Nameh*. Although it took Firdausi thirty years to finish the epic, it was not until after his death that Mahmud sent the promised reward for his accomplishment.

This epic is a collection of smaller epics in which many of the Persian kings' lives are retold. The principal hero, Rustem, called the Persian Hercules, is celebrated for his many exploits and great nobility. The minor heroes in the *Shah-Nameh* are also endowed with courage, cunning, and strength above that of ordinary men.

Firdausi uses the theme of love at first sight throughout the epic. Here is a description of Tahmineh, the heroine, when she first comes to Rustem:

A moon-faced beauty rose upon his sight,
Like the sparkling sun, full of bloom and fragrance;

Her eye-brows bended like the archer's bow,
Her ringlets fateful as the warrior's kamund;
And graceful as the lofty cypress tree,
She moved toward the champion, who surprised
At this enchanting vision, asked the cause
Which brought her thither. Softly thus she spoke:—
"I am the daughter of the king, my name
Tahmineh, no one from behind the screen
Of privacy has yet beheld me, none;
Nor even heard the echo of my voice.
But I have heard of thy prodigious deeds,
Of thy unequaled valor and renown. . . ."
(Atkinson, p. 123)

James Atkinson, the translator, states in his preface that the ancient Persians believed completely in this method of finding a mate.

Summary

Although Firdausi mentions many Persian kings, his is primarily concerned with Rustem, who at birth appears to be a year old. When only a boy, Rustem shows his courage by battling a white elephant that is killing his people. He slays it with one mighty blow of his mace.

Later, while Rustem is visiting a neighboring kingdom, Tahmineh, the king's daughter, falls in love with him. She comes secretly in the night, tells him she has sworn to love no other, and begs him to ask for her hand. The two are married and Tahmineh becomes pregnant, but Rustem has to return to his own country, and Tahmineh raises their son Sohrab alone. Rustem does not learn that he has a son, for Tahmineh tells him the baby was a girl.

When Sohrab grows up he decides to seek his father. Although only fourteen years old, he already has a reputation as a formidable warrior, and he joins the army that his father Rustem is opposing. The two meet on the battlefield, and Rustem gives Sohrab a mortal wound before Sohrab reveals his identity. When Tahmineh hears of this tragedy, she throws herself into a fire.

Rustem is later killed through the treachery of the king of Kabul, who digs pits in the road Rustem is to take and covers them with bushes. Rustem falls into one and dies.

Firdausi ends his epic with an invocation in which he asks the blessing of his king-protector Mahmud.

Zana Easley

The Song of Roland

The origin of this eighth-century French epic is obscure, but the story is based on a battle between the Gascons of Spain and Charlemagne of France. Einhard, an early biographer of Charlemagne, says in his account, "In this battle Egginhard the royal seneschal, Anselm the Count of the Palace, and Hruodland (Roland), the Warden of Breton Marches, were killed, with very many others." (quoted in Merwin, p. viii) This is the first mention we have of the knight who was to be eulogized in one of the greatest epics of the Middle Ages.

Charlemagne had occupied a number of Spanish cities, but the city of Saragossa and its Moslem leader Marsiliun would not surrender to the Christian French. After seven years Charlemagne disbanded his Spanish campaign, gathered his troops, and left for home. Why he did so is uncertain, but it seems probable that most of the Spanish were more willing to be under Moslem rule than to be "rescued" by Charlemagne; consequently, although they tolerated his presence in their cities, they did not particularly welcome his victories. While Charlemagne's army was retreating through a narrow pass in the Pyrenees, the rear guard was ambushed by Gascons and massacred. It is upon this incident that the *Song of Roland* is based.

The epic glorifies Christianity, but among the early Christians of Western Europe it was generally believed that "pagans" should be either converted or killed. Even Archbishop Turpin, a man of God, kills pagans without thinking he has committed a sin. In the epic Christianity provides the moral justification for Charlemagne's campaign, but in actuality his motives were not entirely religious. Undoubtedly the spread of Christianity also meant the growth of his empire.

Courage and honor are the most important values in *Roland*. Ganelon, Roland's step-father, lacks both and is suitably punished; Roland demonstrates both throughout, but he also suffers from pride. Even when surrounded and outnumbered by his enemies, he hesitates until the last possible moment to summon Charlemagne, feeling that it is more noble to fight valiantly against all odds. Only when he is certainly defeated does he blow his ivory horn:

> Count Roland's mouth with running blood is red;
> He's burst asunder the temples of his head;
> He sounds his horn in anguish and distress.
> King Carlon hears, and so do all the French.
> Then said the King, "This horn is long of breath."
> " 'Tis blown," quoth Naimon, "with all a brave man's
>   strength." (Sayers, p. 120)

The primary poetic device of the epic is assonance. Each stanza, or *laisse,* is composed of a group of lines, varying in number, all ending with the same vowel sound. The shift from one set of sounds to another sets up a rhythmic pattern that emphasizes the movement from one incident to the next in the narrative.

Summary

As the *Song of Roland* opens, the Spanish city of Saragossa has been resisting the advances of the French army of Charlemagne for seven years. Marsiliun, the Moslem ruler of the city, devises a plan that he hopes will rid him of Charlemagne. He offers Charlemagne great riches and promises to meet him in France to be converted to Christianity. As surety, Marsiliun says he will send some of his best men as hostages.

A messenger arrives at Charlemagne's camp bearing Marsiliun's offer. Charlemagne decides to accept it and, at Roland's suggestion, he names Ganelon, Roland's step-father, to ride back to Saragossa and accept the gifts. Ganelon, fearing danger to his life, asks if someone else cannot be sent. Roland jeers at Ganelon's cowardice and offers to go in his place, but Charlemagne refuses and orders Ganelon to obey.

Ganelon is furious. He hates and envies Roland, who has gained Charlemagne's favor by his bravery in battle. Upon reaching Saragossa he asks for Marsiliun's help to betray Roland. The Moslem leader is so delighted with this opportunity that he rewards Ganelon with many gifts.

The plot to kill Roland is this: Charlemagne is to be persuaded to leave Roland in command of a small rear guard while he leads the rest of his army into France. As soon as the troops have left, Marsiliun will attack the almost defenseless Roland.

Ganelon returns to the French camp with the riches Marsiliun has given him and makes his proposal to Charlemagne. Roland, ever willing to serve his king, agrees to command the rear guard, and Ganelon's trap is set. That night Charlemagne dreams that the entire rear guard will be annihilated by the Moslems. The next morning he wakes troubled, but decides he can do nothing and goes on.

As soon as Charlemagne is out of the way, Marsiliun attacks. Roland vanquishes many pagans with his mighty sword Durendal, but his men are outnumbered. Finally, after a great many of his friends have been killed, he blows his ivory horn as a signal to Charlemagne. The king, afar off, recognizes it and turns back, but he is too late to save Roland.

Charlemagne now realizes that Ganelon is a traitor, has him tortured, and then turns his attention to the Moslems. Marsiliun has been injured by Roland and his army weakened, and he is relying on his African allies for help. There is a fierce battle when they arrive, but Charlemagne takes Saragossa. Marsiliun dies, and his wife Bramimunde is carried to France with Charlemagne to become a Christian.

Ganelon is put on trial and, although thirty members of his family attest to his honesty, he is found guilty and sentenced to be drawn and quartered. The thirty members of his family are hanged. When Charlemagne is petitioned by Saint Gabriel to aid a neighboring king who has been beseiged by pagans, he exclaims, "Oh, God, my life is a burden!"

Zana Easley

El Cid

The Spanish epic *El Cantar de Mio Cid*—the Poem of the Cid—was written about 1140. Its hero, Don Rodrigo (or Ruy) Diaz de Vivar, was a real person who had died about fifty years before. He had been an outstanding fighter in the Spanish wars against the Moors and so had won the title of El Cid Campeador—the Warrior Lord. He soon became a folk hero, and his deeds were celebrated in this poem and later in the historical narrative *Cronica del Cid*.

The epic is quite short, about one-fourth the length of the *Iliad,* and deals with only a part of the Cid's life. Other parts have been used by other authors, the best known being that of the French playwright Corneille, who dramatized an earlier episode of Ruy Diaz's life in his play *Le Cid*.

The Cid is referred to throughout the epic as "he who in good hour was born." A hero who appears to have no faults, he is always courteous and brave, beloved by the people. His only troubles come from the jealously of those less noble than he. He is deeply religious and, together with his wife and his followers, often prays for God's aid in overcoming his enemies. One of the Cid's physical characteristics is his fine beard, which he often mentions with pride.

An important value in this epic is honor. It grows from the recognition of noble deeds and demands a due respect. Material wealth is one sign of this recognition. The Cid is rewarded for his military victories with gifts of money and land; conversely, the Heirs of Carrion are punished for their treachery by having to forfeit wealth, as well as by being defeated in combat. The Cid's honor is also emphasized by the loyalty of his followers, the devotion of his wife, and the beauty and purity of his daughters. When they are injured, it is a direct insult to him; when they are married, his honor increases according to their husbands' status:

The wedding is performed   of Doña Elvira and Doña Sol;
the first marriage was noble   but this much more so.

To greater honour he weds them   than was theirs before.
See how he grows in honour   who in good hour was born,
his daughters are wives of the Kings   of Navarre and
    Aragon.
Now the Kings of Spain   are his kinsmen,
and all advance in honour   through my Cid the Cam-
    peador. (Merwin, p. 240)

Summary

The epic begins by celebrating the heroic deeds of the Cid. Although he has performed nobly in battle for King Alfonso, others are envious of his success and, by lying, persuade the king to banish him. He spends three years in exile, fighting Alfonso's enemies. Finally his friends persuade the king to repeal his banishment, and the Cid is welcomed back. The king arranges for the marriage of the Cid's daughters to the Heirs of Carrion, and the Cid accepts this favor because of the honor it does him, even though he has some personal misgivings. Later his sons-in-law show themselves to be cowards in his presence. Humiliated, they vow to humiliate the Cid in retaliation. So they arrange to take their wives on a journey to Carrion. On the way they stop in a lonely place, strip the ladies, and beat them until they are bloody and senseless. The Heirs then leave them for dead in the Oak-Wood of Corpes.

Fortunately the ladies are found by one of the Cid's loyal kinsmen. Their husbands are discovered, forced to return their dowries, and vanquished in battle by the Cid's challengers, thus giving him satisfaction. The epic ends with the second marriage of the two daughters, this time to the kings of Navarre and Aragon. Since these husbands are of higher status than the others, the marriage is an even greater honor for the Cid.

Margaret Fleming

The Lay of Igor's Campaign

The *Lay of Igor's Campaign* is the single literary masterpiece of the Kievan period of Russian history. This work, unlike most epics, was not sung. Although the author is anonymous, he was probably attached to the court and undoubtedly was familiar with both oral and literary poetic traditions. The great originality of his work is that he applied methods of oral poetry to a written epic.

The epic is marked by obscurities and inconsistencies, for only one copy of it survived until 1800, and that was partially destroyed by fire in 1812 when Napoleon invaded Russia. Some passages were reconstructed from memory, but others have never been satisfactorily explained. The fact that the original language was an archaic form of Russian has added to the difficulties of translation.

The *Lay* tells of Prince Igor's attempt to expel the Kumans, a nomadic tribe, from southern Russia. After initial success, he is defeated and captured; with divine help he escapes to return home. The author cites many examples of discord in Russia and uses Igor's experiences, even though unsuccessful, as a vehicle to encourage the Russians to forget their differences and unite against their common enemies.

The plot of this epic is extremely simple and the character of the hero is undeveloped. Its great strength lies in the poetry of its language. The author shows acute perception of natural beauty and uses vivid descriptions to show how Nature aids Igor. He also links war with more familiar experience in a way reminiscent of Homer:

> On the river Nemiga they built haystacks of heads.
> They are threshed with steel flails
> and lives are left behind on the threshing floor.
> Souls abandon their bodies.
> The bloody shores of the river Nemiga
>   were sown with misfortune,
>   were strewn with the bones of Russia's sons.
>   (Zenkovsky, p. 155)

Summary

This epic begins by recalling an early bard named Boyan, who was evidently attached to the court of Igor's father Sviatoslav. The author implies that he will not "soar above" his story, as Boyan did with his tales of earlier Russian princes.

Igor and his brother Vsevolod seek fame and glory by trying to expel the Kumans from southern Russia. Just as they are ready to set out on their campaign, an eclipse of the sun throws a shadow over their troops. (An actual eclipse did occur on May 1, 1185.) The Russians perceive this as an evil omen and are frightened. Igor, however, inspires his men to continue.

Igor's campaign is marked by other evil omens. His father Sviatoslav dreams that his son has been captured and laments for him, but he also blames Igor for not accepting help from his father. Igor's wife also laments for her husband, fearing she will never see him again.

The omens are fulfilled: Igor is unsuccessful and he is captured by the Kumans. God, however, sees fit to have him escape, and Nature helps him in his flight. No birds sing; "only the woodpeckers in the osciers climbing, with taps marked the way to the river for Igor." (Nabokov, p. 69)

Everyone rejoices at Igor's return because Russia without Igor would be like a body without a head. The tale ends with an exhortation for all Christians to join together in a battle to free Russia of the pagans.

Zana Easley

The Nibelungenlied

The medieval Germanic epic *Das Nibelungenlied* takes its name from the mythical Nibelungs, guardians of a great treasure. Much of the material is legendary, though some characters and incidents are historical. The first part of the poem deals with the journey of Siegfried to Burgundy, his wooing and wedding of Kriemhild, and his death. The second tells of the wooing and wedding of Kriemhild by King Etzel (Attila the Hun) and of her subsequent revenge upon Hagen, the slayer of Siegfried. In each section there are parallel motifs—expeditions, celebrations, and betrayals—that unify the epic structurally. Thematically it is unified by the continuing hostility between Kriemhild and Hagen.

Although Siegfried has the qualities of an epic hero—strength, courage, magical powers—he does not triumph; rather he is killed at the midpoint of the story. Perhaps Kriemhild should be considered an epic heroine, a position unique to this poem.

The forms of Christianity are important to the action of the narrative, especially in the second part, where Kriemhild hesitates to marry King Etzel because he is a pagan. Ironically, the characters' motivation is often at odds with Christian principles; a prime example is the prominence of Kriemhild's pursuit of vengeance:

> "I cannot show you mercy—my heart has none to show!" said Etzel's queen. "Hagen of Troneck has done me so much wrong that there can be no reconciliation as long as I live! You must all pay for it together." (Hatto, p. 260)

Little is known about the author of the *Nibelungenlied*. Possibly he was a clergyman; he may have been a minstrel attached to the household of some Austrian nobleman. Whatever his status, he was undoubtedly familiar with court life, for he describes it in great detail. Clothing, as a status symbol, is emphasized throughout:

> The ladies were well supplied with the best Moroccan and Libyan silk that a royal family ever acquired, and Kriemhild let it be seen clearly that these knights enjoyed her favour. And now that they had set their hearts on this voyage with its lofty goal, furs of ermine no longer seemed

> good enough: their linings were covered instead with
> coal-black brocades all spangled with brilliant stones set
> in Arabian gold such as would well become brave warriors
> on festive occasions today. (Hatto, p. 57)

The rituals of feasting, tournaments, and church-going are also ex-
plicitly portrayed. Moreover, the work is almost a manual of court
etiquette in its advice on such matters as how a nobleman ought to
reward his vassals. The profusion of such details enriches the poem
and gives us a vivid picture of life in the Middle Ages.

Summary

Siegfried, the young prince of the Netherlands, through
many trials proves himself a fearless knight. He has won the treasure
of the Nibelungs, including a cloak which confers invisibility on its
wearer. Siegfried journeys to Burgundy, where he successfully woos
the lovely princess Kriemhild. Before he can marry her, however,
he has to help her brother Gunther win Brunhild, the warrior queen.
Although she consents to marry Gunther, Brunhild is so proud of
her physical strength that Gunther is afraid she will never submit to
him. He asks Siegfried to take his place on their wedding night.
Wearing the cloak of invisibility, Siegfried overcomes Brunhild for
Gunther. He departs unrecognized, leaving a ring with her. Years
later, Siegfried's wife Kriemhild provokes strife when she taunts
Brunhild with the story, citing Siegfried's ring as proof.

As a result of Brunhild's hostility, Gunther and his knight
Hagen bring about Siegfried's death. Hagen discovers the one place
where Siegfried is vulnerable and kills him. He then takes the
Nibelung treasure and sinks it in the Rhine.

With her husband dead and her treasure stolen, Kriemhild
is wretched in her grief and frustration but is powerless to avenge
Siegfried's death. She lives, a lonely widow, at Gunther's court until
King Etzel of Hungary asks for her hand in marriage. After much
persuasion Kriemhild agrees to marry him, seeing in this course
a way to strengthen her position.

Kriemhild and Etzel live happily for some years and have
a son. Then Kriemhild begins to think about Siegfried again and
makes plans for her revenge. She pleads with her husband until he
allows her to invite Gunther and Hagen to Hungary. They accept
and start out on the journey. Although a water-sprite tries to dis-
suade Hagen from crossing the Rhine, he disregards the omen and
continues on the trip.

This excursion results in a terrible war in which many
noble knights of both sides are slain. Kriemhild finally gains her
revenge when she murders both Hagen and her brother Gunther.

She, in turn, is killed by one of Etzel's men. Thus a whole family is annihilated, and the treasure of the Nibelungs is lost forever.

Zana Easley

The Kalevala

Kalevala means land of the sons of Kaleva, a mythological Finnish hero, and hence Finland. This epic is a composite of Finnish folk tales, songs, and stories, in which the people have preserved the memory of their sacred groves and legendary heroes. Although many of the stories date back to before the twelfth century, they were first brought together in 1831 by Dr. Elias Lönnrot, a country physician. He first called the collection *Kantele* (harp), but after more research changed it to its present name, publishing the final version in 1849.

The *Kalevala* tells of several semidivine heroes who share the characteristics of courage and intelligence. It preserves creation myths, nature stories, and myths of evil. Lemminkainen's descent to the underworld—Tuonela—is similar to such stories in the classical epics. The birth of a son called the King of Karelia to the virgin Marjatta has been interpreted as a symbol of Christianity overcoming paganism in Finland.

The epic is rich in descriptions of nature that evoke the far northern setting:

> He drove along the ages, rustling in the reeds. In the summer he swung in swamps, and in the winter roared in pines, crackled in birches, and snapped in alder bushes. (Johnson, p. 176)

Another interesting characteristic is the metallic imagery found throughout the work:

> This was the iron-fisted man, black as iron to look upon. He wore a stony helmet on his head, stone shoes, and carried at his waist a golden knife with a handle of many-colored copper. (Johnson, p. 121)

This, of course, indicates its importance in the culture of the Finns.

Summary

Beginning with the creation of the world by Ilmatar, the daughter of the wind, the epic tells of the life of her son Vainamoinen, the first of the brave race of singers. His powerful song makes the earth tremble and the heaven storm.

Vainamoinen lives a long time on the meadows of Vainola, charming his people with his songs. When he is old, a young Laplander named Joukahainen challenges him to a duel of magic verses. At first Vainamoinen will not accept, but when the youth insults him, he sings and the earth shakes. Joukahainen then finds himself in a swamp up to his chin. He begs Vainamoinen to release him, offering all sorts of riches, but the old magician cannot be swayed until the youth promises him the hand of his young sister Aino in marriage. At this, Vainamoinen releases him, because he wants a companion in his age.

When Joukahainen tells his family of his promise, his mother is delighted, but his sister Aino is inconsolable. Finally, seeing no alternative, she kills herself by walking into the sea.

Another hero of the epic is the mighty smith Ilmarinen. He forges a magic Sampo, a mill that grinds wheat, money, and salt, for Louhi, the sorceress of the far north, so that he can marry her daughter. Later, after his wife's death, he and Vainamoinen and a young hero named Lemminkainen journey together to rescue the Sampo from Louhi. Their success brings good fortune to their people.

The epic ends with the birth of a child to a virgin, Marjatta. Her son succeeds Vainamoinen as the great singer, and Vainamoinen, displaced, sails off in a copper boat.

Zana Easley

References

Atkinson, James, trans. *The Shah-Nameh,* by Abdul Kasim Firdausi. London: Frederick Warne and Co., 1886.
Hatto, Arthur Thomas, trans. *The Nibelungenlied.* Baltimore: Penguin Books, 1969.
Johnson, Aili Kolehmainen, trans. *Kalevala,* by Elias Lönnrot. Hancock, Mich.: The Book Concern, 1950.
Merwin, William S., trans. *Poem of the Cid.* New York: New American Library, Mentor Books, 1959.
———. *The Song of Roland.* New York: Random House, Vintage Books, 1963.
Nabokov, Vladimir, trans. *Song of Igor's Campaign.* New York: Random House, Vintage Books, 1960.
Sayers, Dorothy L., trans. *The Song of Roland.* Baltimore: Penguin Books, 1957.
Wright, David, trans. *Beowulf.* Baltimore: Penguin Books, 1957.
Zenkovsky, Serge, ed. *Medieval Russia's Epics, Chronicles, and Tales.* New York: E. P. Dutton and Co., 1963.

Renaissance Epics

These four works are the most notable examples of Renaissance epic:

Orlando Furioso, by Ludovico Ariosto, 1516—Italian
The Lusiads, by Luis vaz de Camoens, 1572—Portuguese
Jerusalem Delivered, by Torquato Tasso, 1581—Italian
The Faerie Queene, by Edmund Spenser, 1596—English

Although the Renaissance epic continued to exert a strong influence for over a century—both upon such major works as Milton's *Paradise Lost* (1667) and such minor works as Voltaire's *Henriade* (1723) — the *Faerie Queene* is usually considered the culminating work of this genre.

Orlando Furioso had predecessors, such as Boiardo's *Orlando Innamorato* (1510), but it was Ariosto who established the hallmarks of the genre, fixing the heroic adventures of a Christian knight as the proper subject matter for such epics. His purpose, however, was not solely to instruct by providing a heroic model; he also introduced many fantastical and mythological elements for his readers' delight as well as profit. His epic is far more luxuriant and romantic than its classical counterparts.

Of the many areas in which Ariosto's influence can be traced, perhaps the most imitated feature is his description of the garden of the enchantress Alcina (VII), which represents the temptation of sensual joys. The later epics of Camoens, Tasso, and Spenser all make use of similar settings.

In the *Lusiads,* Camoens climaxes his combination of historical events, classical epic machinery, and allegorical episodes with a vision of Venus' Isle of Love. Here the garden with its sensual enjoyments is a reward for the conquering heroes and a glorious projection of the future. Camoens apparently did not feel the same obligation to stress the dangers inherent in sensuality as did the other writers of the period. He was, however, criticized for his excesses, and the

garden scene, as well as other "pagan" sections of the poem, was often
expurgated.

In *Jerusalem Delivered,* Tasso attempts to play down the
magical and supernatural elements he had decried in Ariosto; nevertheless, he uses manipulation by archangels and devils. In line with
the high seriousness of his Christian design, his Gardens of Armida
symbolize the menace of sensuality to a Christian knight. Still the
menace is described so lovingly, and the portrayal is so alluring, that,
under the threat of orthodox criticism, the unfortunate Tasso tried
almost immediately to recall his work. In later editions, he attempted
to subjugate the garden scene more firmly to his didactic purpose.

In Spenser's *Faerie Queene,* the pull from these two directions—the didactic and the sensual—is apparent. While Spenser shares
Tasso's concern for the seriousness of the poetic function, particularly
in celebrating Christian heroism, he is equally inclined toward the
delightful possibilities of poetry. He too adapts the enchantress' garden as a symbol of sin in Acrasia's Bower of Bliss, although in this
poem the didacticism is almost submerged in the power and beauty
of the imagery.

Orlando Furioso

Orlando Furioso is perhaps the best example of the Renaissance chivalric epic. Its antecedent is the fifteenth century chivalric
romance *Orlando Innamorato* by Boiardo. Many of the characters
of the *Furioso* are first introduced in the *Innamorato,* but they are
developed more fully by Ariosto.

The work is a skillful mixture of historical, fantastical, and
autobiographical elements. Its ironic tone reflects Ariosto's awareness that the chivalric world was, at its supposed height, already a
beautiful impossibility. The irony is consistent, whether Ariosto is
speaking in his own voice to his love, Alessandra Benucci, or com-
menting as an author on the effects of love upon Orlando:

> If she, who to like cruel pass has well
> Nigh brought my feeble wit which fain would climb
> And hourly wastes my sense, concede me skill
> And strength my daring promise to fulfill (I. ii. Rose, p. 3)

Recognition of the defeat of the chivalric code is implicit even in
those moments which ostensibly prove its worth, as in the battle for
Paris. The effect is a sense of melancholic regret for a world which
perhaps never was, but should have been.

Ottava rima had already been established as the poetic
form for Italian romance, but in Ariosto's hands it became more
powerful and more ironic than ever before. Although the shifts in

the narrative are sometimes confusing or awkward as Ariosto stops
to pursue a subplot, he maintains a satisfying sense of progression in
the work.

The basic narrative is embroidered with various motifs.
Some of these are apparently intended to demonstrate the proper function of chivalry. Others examine different kinds of love—spiritual
and sensual—both of which are combined in the idealized love of
Rogero and Bradamante. The inclusion of many such incidents gives
the work an exuberance and a richness of texture not found in the
typical medieval epic.

Summary

Orlando Furioso begins with a statement that closely imitates Virgil's *Aeneid:* "Of loves and ladies, knights and arms, I
sing. . . ." The situation is the ninth-century siege of Paris by the
Saracens, with the Christian forces led by the renowned Charlemagne.
The Saracen maiden Angelica is sent by her father to spread disunion
among the Christian knights; she does so most effectively by capturing
the hearts of Orlando (Roland) and several others. In this epic
Orlando demonstrates not only the heroic ferocity of the hero of the
Song of Roland, but also the romantic characteristics of the Arthurian
lover.

When Angelica weds the Saracen knight Medoro, an ob-
vious inferior to Orlando, he is maddened by his passion into a frenzy—
becoming *furioso*. The result is not only neglect of his knightly duties
for the service of love—which Charlemagne has decried—but an ab-
dication of his honor in the pursuit of it.

His friend Astolfo journeys to the under and then to the
upper world to recover Orlando's wits. He is successful, and Orlando,

> Thus being to his former wits restored,
> He was likewise delivered clean from love. . . .
> (XXXIX. Harrington, p. 347)

With Orlando restored to action, the Christian army captures Biserta easily; the Saracen champions Agrmant, Gradoso, and
Brandimart are slain, and the death of Rodomont at Rogero's hand
establishes the Christian primacy, as well as the founding of the
House of Este, Ariosto's patrons.

Lois Mervyn

The Lusiads

The *Lusiads,* an "epic poem of commerce," is different both
in intent and tone from other Renaissance epics. It celebrates not the

personal valor of a single hero but the collective achievement of a nation. Camoens' glorification of Portuguese commercial accomplishments, however, is not allegorized with complete success. The work is filled with maritime and pastoral imagery, catalogs of armor, and descriptions of royal splendor; such rhetorical devices as epic similes and apostrophes to the muses clearly attempt to exalt the subject to epic proportions. But by making his protagonist a relatively recent historical figure, Camoens loses some of the charm of antiquity and much of the license for embroidery conferred by more remote subjects. Moreover, his allusions to contemporary figures are often labored and his grandiloquent style cumbersome.

The poem is of historical interest because it dramatizes the impetus toward exploration that was current in Europe at the time. Its publication evoked widespread response. Within thirty years the *Lusiads* had been translated eight times into four different languages. The work also provides the modern reader with insight into the political climate of Europe. An example is this comment on Italy's fall from classical glory:

> While Holy Faith's hereditary foes
> Possess the treasures where Cynifio flows;
> And all secure, behold their harvests smile
> In waving gold along the banks of Nile.
> And thou, O lost to glory, lost to fame,
> And dark oblivion of thy ancient name,
> By every vicious luxury debased,
> Each noble passion from the breast erased,
> Nerveless in sloth, enfeebling arts thy boast,
> Oh, Italy, how fallen, how low, how lost! (Mickle, p. 265)

Camoens' consciousness of the role of poetry and the relationship of the poet to history is shown in the several digressions upon such subjects. Although he was a soldier-poet in the best tradition of the Renaissance, his poetic gift was simply not on the level of Spenser or even Ariosto. But if his work will not stand in the first rank of the period's epics, it is still an interesting historical document.

Summary

The Lusiads are sons of Lusus, the mythical founder of Portugal. This epic celebrates their conquest of India. The poem opens with a council of the gods, called by Jove to decide the fate of the explorer Vasco da Gama. They all, with the exception of Bacchus, agree with Venus' proposal to support him.

After suitable invocations Gama's forces sail for India by way of the Cape of Good Hope. At Mombasa, in what is now Kenya, they first encounter and overcome Moorish opposition. With the intervention of the gods they continue to win battles with the Moors. Farther north along the African coast they make friends with the King of Malindi, who controls the passage to India. He gives them aid and supplies them with a pilot, thus insuring their eventual foothold in India and success in further exploration.

Here the narrative is interrupted by a flashback that fills in some of the historical background of this venture. Camoens includes accounts of warring factions, court intrigues, and battles for the provinces, as well as the tragic story of Doña Inez and Don Pedro. This section culminates in the fleet's departure in 1497. Such switching back and forth in time and space is characteristic of Camoens' narrative technique.

Once established in India, Gama consolidates the Portuguese holding. His men penetrate the Indian peninsula and battle the Moors and the Turks. While these actions are going on, back in Portugal Almeyda is appointed the first Viceroy of India. His appointment is a further step in the movement toward empire.

From the time the Portuguese ally themselves with the Indian ruler Zamorim, there is no doubt that their campaign in India will be successful. Almeyda's victory over the combined Indian and Turkish forces, together with the Duke of Albuquerque's conquest of Malacca, secures the Portuguese position.

The historical setting is now abandoned for the allegorical, as Venus takes the heroic Lusiads to her Isle of Love. There they see a vision of the entire world as the scene of future glories for their race. The poem ends with an exhortation to the present king, Sebastian, to consolidate and preserve Portugal's former glories.

Lois Mervyn

Jerusalem Delivered

Jerusalem Delivered is the last great work of the Italian Renaissance. In it Tasso attempts to fuse heroic epic and chivalric romance into a new literary form, rivaling the classical epic. The intellectual climate of the period encouraged consideration of the relationship between poetry and moral issues.

Tasso said he wanted to write a noble and delightful poem that would avoid the fanciful supernaturalism of Ariosto's epic. He believed that a work of art should embody moral instruction, so he chose the siege and capture of Jerusalem in 1099 by Godfrey of Boulogne as an appropriate epic subject for the theme of Christian militancy triumphant.

Although Tasso had expressed disapproval of the supernatural, his work retains some flavor of the marvelous in its use of

enchantments and divine intervention and in the exotic splendor of
the pagan characters. These elements add color to the historical
events depicted. In fact, many critics believe that the poem succeeds
because of the romantic rather than the strictly epic components.

Tasso portrays certain psychological aspects of love rarely
touched upon in other epics. For example, here is his analysis of the
enchantress Armida:

> She ran, nor of her honor took regard
>   (Oh where be all her vaunts and triumphs now?
> Love's empire great of late she made or mar'd,
>   To her his subjects humbly bend and bow,
> And with her pride mix'd was a scorn so hard,
>   That to be lov'd she lov'd; yet whilst they woo,
> Her lovers all she hates; that pleas'd her will,
> To conquer men, and conquer'd, so to kill) :
>   (Fairfax, p. 326)

Tasso is also remarkable for his depiction of the heroism of failure and
his sensitivity to the horrifying rather than the heroic elements of
violence. His approach is therefore more congenial to the modern
temperament than that of most other Renaissance writers.

Summary

Godfrey of Boulogne receives a heavenly commission to
recapture Jerusalem from the pagans. The pagan king Aladine, preparing to resist, seizes a statue of the Virgin, which is subsequently
stolen from his mosque. In retaliation he orders a wholesale slaughter
of the Christian population of Jerusalem. This fate is averted by
the intended sacrifice of Sophronia and her lover Olindo, but before
the sacrifice can take place they are rescued by the pagan warrior
maiden Clorinda.

Negotiations for settlement fail and both sides prepare for
battle. In the first assault on the city walls one of the Christian
princes is killed. Satan sends his angels on earth to intervene, with
the result that the enchantress Armida attempts to seduce the Christian
knights *en masse*. Although Godfrey rejects her false pleas for assistance, she does manage to attract a small company of knights. Two
of the foremost Christian warriors become rivals for her love and
desert Godfrey.

The Egyptian leader Argantes sends a challenge to the
Christians for single combat. The knight Tancred accepts it, but
when his beloved Erminia fails to arrive at his camp, he deserts to
seek her. On the way he encounters the pagan Rambaldo, a former
Christian knight who has followed Armida.

Meanwhile Argantes renews his challenge. The Christian knights, shamed by Tancred's absence, eventually send Raimond. By the intervention of enchanters, Raimond is seriously wounded, and the Christians are driven back with heavy losses.

The battle goes on. Clorinda, the pagan champion, and Godfrey, the Christian, both show their bravery. Clorinda is finally killed—but she is converted on her deathbed by the returned and repentant Tancred.

The Christian forces grow weaker, plagued by mutiny, demonic intervention, and drought. Finally they receive a divine sign— rain. Godfrey is transported to Heaven where, in a vision, he is given assurance of eventual success.

Meanwhile Rinaldo, one of the Christian heroes who had deserted to Armida, has been imprisoned in her palace and garden. When he is released from her spell, Armida's love turns to hatred. She incites pagans to pursue and fight him. Rinaldo is victorious and returns to the Christian camp, contrite and strengthened. He spearheads the Christian storming of Jerusalem and the ensuing slaughter of the pagans. This episode symbolizes the debilitating effect of sensual love, which must be overcome by a Christian knight before he can fulfill his duty.

During the battle for Jerusalem, Tancred and Argantes meet on the wall, and Argantes is slain. Erminia is then discovered in the train of the retreating pagans; she revives the almost-dead Tancred.

The final battle with the Egyptians occurs the following morning. Many champions on both sides are slain. The wicked Armida flees but is pursued and converted by Rinaldo. The poem ends with the army marshaled at the Holy Sepulchre to give thanks for the liberation of Jerusalem.

Lois Mervyn

The Faerie Queene

The *Faerie Queene* is the culmination of the Renaissance epic. Though Spenser imitates the structure and some of the conventions of the classical epics, he owes much more to Ariosto and Tasso. While the poem resembles *Orlando Furioso* in the luxuriant variety of its characters and incidents, its high seriousness is more like Tasso's. Spenser also drew inspiration from medieval romance for much of his material and from the morality plays for his allegory. His language is deliberately archaic, echoing Chaucer, and his hero, Prince Arthur (later King Arthur), is staunchly British. This diverse mixture of elements is unified by the setting—Fairy Land, with its Queen Gloriana—and by the presence of Arthur in each book.

Initially Spenser had planned to compose twelve books, each exemplifying one moral virtue. This ambitious task was only slightly more than half completed at his death. Generations of readers and critics, however, have found ample material for discussion in the work's multiple levels of interpretation.

The plot recounts the adventures of courageous knights rescuing damsels in distress, patterned after the *Morte D'Arthur* and using Arthur himself as a primary character. But, even on the superficial level it is obvious that the work is an allegory with such characters as Despair, Envy, and Slander playing significant roles. Spenser indicates character traits by using foreign words in the names Una (truth), Sansfoy (faithlessness), Sansloy (lawlessness), Sansjoy (joylessness), Alma (the soul), and many others. The names of various castles also indicate their symbolic significance. This moral allegory, however, is only one of several levels.

The characters of the *Faerie Queene* may also be masks for Biblical presentations. Book I, for example, has been interpreted as an enactment of the Fall of Man. The Red Cross knight—representing Adam—is tempted by Duessa—Eve—to step into the snares of Orgoglio—Satan; but through the intervention of Arthur—Christ—he is freed from the consequences of his actions.

Another level of interpretation involves the whole scope of English history and politics. Because Spenser believed that the Church of England was the true church, evil characters can often be associated with Catholicism and good characters with loyal Protestants. Thus the witch Duessa, tried by Queen Mercilla, represents Mary Queen of Scots being tried by Queen Elizabeth. The giant Orgoglio is Philip II of Spain; Belphoebe, the chaste huntress, is Queen Elizabeth; and Timias, her lover, is Sir Walter Raleigh. Queen Elizabeth also appears in the poem in the person of Britomart, the chaste warrior maiden. Queen Belge, rescued by Artegall in Book V, represents the Low Countries oppressed by Spain; and the victimized Queen Irena, rescued by Arthur, is Ireland. This level of interpretation is lost on most contemporary readers, especially Americans, but it was vital to the poem at the time of its creation.

The Spenserian stanza, invented for this poem, consists of nine lines, rhyming *ababbcbcc*, all iambic pentameter, except the last, which has an extra foot. This line creates the effect of a pause at the end of each stanza. The rhythm thus produced, as well as the internal music of alliteration, assonance, and onomatopoeia, are illustrated in the following passage:

And more, to lulle him in his slumber soft,
   A trickling stream from high rocke tumbling downe
And ever-drizling raine upon the loft,
   Mixt with a murmuring winde, much like the sowne

> Of swarming Bees, did cast him in a swowne:
> No other noyse, nor peoples troublous cryes,
> As still are wont t'annoy the walled towne,
> Might there be heard: but carelesse Quiet lyes,
> Wrapt in eternall silence farre from enemyes.
>   (*Faerie Queene,* I: I. 41)

The craftsmanship here shown, together with vivid sensuous imagery and an almost flawless form, gives this poem a unique charm and helps explain why Spenser is called "the poet's poet."

Summary

In Book I, Gloriana sends the Red Cross knight, symbol of Holiness, to slay a dragon beseiging the castle of Una, embodiment of truth. With Una's help the knight defeats Error in his first conquest, but Archimago, an evil magician, turns him against Una and leads him to champion Duessa, a witch disguised as a beautiful maiden. Two of her companions, Lucifera and the giant Orgoglio, tempt him and cast him into a dungeon. Una hears of his plight and solicits the aid of Prince Arthur, who frees him and slays Orgoglio. The knight resumes his mission but is almost defeated by Despair. Una then takes him to the House of Holiness, where he is revived. After this he kills the dragon and is betrothed to Una. He is revealed as Saint George, the patron saint of England.

Sir Guyon, Champion of Temperance, is the hero of Book II, and his assignment from Gloriana is to destroy Acrasia, an enchantress who lures men into her Bower of Bliss and turns them into beasts. Fortified by the principles of the Golden Mean, Guyon defeats the wrathful brothers Pyrocles and Cymochles and overcomes the temptations of Phaedria, a beautiful follower of Acrasia. Mammon unsuccessfully tempts him with great wealth. Weakened by this trial, he is rescued by Prince Arthur, who takes him to the House of Alma—the soul—to recover. He is then able to destroy the Bower of Bliss.

Book III is a complex treatment of Chastity. Its heroine is Britomart, a warrior maiden, but Spenser introduces many other characters, such as Belphoebe, a chaste huntress, and Florimell, a lovely maiden pursued by numerous would-be seducers, in order to illustrate different aspects of his theme. Britomart is in love with a mysterious knight, Artegal, who has been revealed to her in a magic mirror. She meets Sir Scudamour, who tells her that his wife Amoret, sister of Belphoebe, has been captured by Busirane, a libertine. Britomart discovers Busirane's castle and destroys it, freeing Amoret.

From these events the theme of Friendship is developed in the following book. Britomart and Amoret become friends after Amoret's rescue, and they set out to find Sir Scudamour. At a tournament many challengers are defeated by a knight in strange disguise. Britomart is challenged and fights to a draw with him. When he splits her helmet and sees her beautiful face, he falls in love with her. As he lifts his visor, Britomart recognizes him as Artegal, and they are betrothed.

Book V is devoted to the exploits of Artegal as champion of Justice. After punishing injustice in several forms, he meets Radigund, Queen of the Amazons, and although he defeats her in battle, he hesitates to kill her because of her beauty. She capitalizes on his weakness and enslaves him. He is saved by Britomart, who kills Radigund without hesitation. After his rescue Artegal joins Arthur, and they vanquish the enemies of Queen Mercilla, a monarch dedicated to peace and justice. While in her company, they witness the trial of the witch Duessa, who has plotted against Mercilla's life. After they restore Queen Belge to her throne, Artegal rescues Irena from a usurper and returns her kingdom to her. He is then attacked by Envy and Despair, supported by the Blatant Beast, Slander.

In Book VI, Gloriana sends Calidore, champion of Courtesy, to capture the Blatant Beast. While in the forest searching for it, Calidore encounters a band of shepherds. He falls in love with Pastorella, a beautiful shepherdess, and joins the band. After a time he captures the Blatant Beast and brings it back in chains, but it escapes to attack all future generations.

The two completed cantos of Book VII, Constancy, introduce Mutability, a titaness who has gained control of the earth and desires to control Heaven. She challenges the authority of Jove, calling him a usurper, but Nature, mother of all the gods, rules against her.

Carolyn Dirksen

References

Fairfax, Edward, trans. *Jerusalem Delivered,* by Torquato Tasso. New York: G. P. Putnam's Sons, 1963.

Harington, John, trans. *Ariosto's Orlando Furioso: Selections from John Harington's Translation.* Bloomington: Indiana University Press, 1969.

Mickle, W. J., trans. *The Lusiads,* by Luis vaz de Camoens. Oxford, 1778.

Rose, William Stewart, trans. *Orlando Furioso,* by Ludovico Ariosto. Indianapolis: Bobbs-Merrill Co., 1968.

Christian Epics—Dante and Milton

Both the *Divine Comedy* of Dante Alighieri and *Paradise Lost* of John Milton transcend nationalism and classical influences to glorify the ideals of Christianity. Dante and Milton followed the classical models and many classical elements are apparent in their epics. Like Virgil they created sophisticated literary epics of outstanding excellence.

It is not too surprising that Dante, writing a Christian epic, followed Virgil, a pagan writer. Virgil had been honored by the medieval Christian church because it was believed that he had prophesied the birth of Christ in one of his short poems (Eclogue IV) written in the first century B.C.

Paradise Lost follows its traditional models not only in form but also in content. Although he is dealing with the Hell and Heaven of Judeo-Christian theology, Milton describes them in classical terms, filling in details omitted in the Scriptures. His descriptions of Pandemonium, the meeting place of the fiends, the Limbo of Vanity, Chaos, and other locations in Hell are reminiscent of similar descriptions in classical epics.

The Divine Comedy

Dante called his work *The Comedy*, not because it was intended to provoke laughter, but because it had a happy ending. The adjective *Divine* was not added to its name until the sixteenth century, but it has been fittingly incorporated, since Dante's subject is the divine plan of God. The epic shows the progress of its hero Dante, as Everyman, from sin through atonement to eternal love. It thus transcends the limits of nationalism to become the celebration of Catholic Christianity.

Although the *Comedy* is entirely comprehensible on the literal level, it is heavily allegorical as well. Abstract qualities are represented by persons, such as Virgil (human reason) and Beatrice (divine love), or by supernatural beings. Every setting, every incident, even the structure of the epic, has allegorical significance.

51

The work is divided into three parts representing the Trinity. Each is designed with careful attention to geographic detail and symbolic correspondence. In each part Dante progresses through concentric circles, moving downward through Hell, upward through Purgatory and Heaven.

The character Virgil, representing human reason, is Dante's guide through Hell and Purgatory, but it is obvious that the author Virgil is Dante's guide in literary matters. Both the structure and the language of the epic show Virgil's influence. For instance, this image of Dante's recalls a very similar one in the *Aeneid:*

> As leaves in autumn loosen and stream down
>   until the branch stands bare above its tatters
>   spread on the rustling ground, so one by one
> the evil seed of Adam in its Fall
>   cast themselves, at his signal, from the shore
>   and streamed away like birds who hear their call.
>   (Ciardi, *Inferno,* p. 45)

Hell, as Dante portrays it, seems to hold more interest for the average reader than either Purgatory or Heaven. The climactic scenes in Heaven all too often seem anticlimactic after the vivid drama of Hell. Is man more wicked than virtuous, or is it just that he is more familiar with evil? Perhaps the answer is literary rather than philosophical. Conflict is more easily made dramatic than divinity.

Dante's Hell is nothing if not dramatic. He depicts sinners and punishments in specific, and often gross, detail. For instance, in this passage the appropriate punishment for flattery is shown:

> Once there, I peered down; and I saw long lines
>   of people in a river of excrement
>   that seemed the overflow of the world's latrines.
> I saw among the felons of that pit
>   one wraith who might or might not have been tonsured—
>   one could not tell, he was so smeared with shit.
>   (Ciardi, *Inferno,* p. 161)

Here the vulgar language fits the subject. In Heaven the language is fittingly exalted:

> That this profound and sacred nature is real
>   the teachings of the evangels, in many places,
>   have stamped on the wax of my mind like a living seal.
>   (Ciardi, *Paradiso,* p. 272)

Dante's integration of subject, setting, and structure shows his virtuosity as a craftsman, but his ability to characterize and the power of his language make him a great artist.

Inferno

Dante awakes in a dark wood and realizes he has lost his way. It is Good Friday. He sees the Mount of Joy and starts to climb it, but the ghost of Virgil appears to him and tells him he can only get there by going through Hell and Purgatory first. Virgil offers to guide him, and they enter Hell through a gate over which is inscribed, "Abandon All Hope, Ye Who Enter Here."

Hell is a huge pit consisting of nine concentric circles arranged in descending levels. Each level is guarded by a monster from classical mythology. The first circle, Limbo, contains the souls of virtuous pagans and unbaptized children. Dante and Virgil go around each circle and then descend to the next lower level.

The farther down they go, the more wicked the sinners they see and the more severe the punishments. God's justice has made the torments correspond to the sins. Thus those who divided kinsmen with discord have their own bodies torn apart; heretics, who perverted theology, are turned upside down in fiery coffins. Dante recognizes many of the damned souls and often stops to talk to them. Some are political leaders recently dead; others are historical or literary figures.

At the very bottom of Hell, Satan is fixed from the waist down in a lake of ice. He has three heads, whose three mouths gnaw Brutus, Cassius, and Judas Iscariot—all betrayers of their masters, the most heinous sin of all. Dante and Virgil, when they reach this level, must climb down along the flank of Satan through the sheet of ice. Suddenly they emerge into open air. They have passed through the earth and come out on the other side. They find themselves looking up at the Mount of Purgatory.

Purgatorio

In the circle that surrounds Purgatory are the souls of the excommunicated and those who postponed repentance. As Dante and Virgil walk around the steep cliffs looking for a way upward, all the souls they meet are astonished to see that Dante casts a shadow. Eventually they find a narrow passageway and begin the difficult climb. At the end of the day Dante grows weary and falls asleep. He wakes to find himself at the gate of Purgatory. Like Hell, it consists of concentric circles. In each circle one of the seven deadly sins is purged away. At the top is the Earthly Paradise. Here Dante meets Beatrice, who has descended from Heaven to be his guide, since Virgil (human reason) can go no further.

Paradiso

It is now Easter Sunday. Dante, led by Beatrice, ascends through the heavens. The first seven spheres are governed by the sun, the moon, and the planets. The eighth heaven is that of the fixed stars, the ninth the Primum Mobile—first mover—and the tenth the Empyrean, at whose center is God. In each sphere Dante sees virtuous souls, saints, and angels. They discourse on various points of philosophy and theology. The epic ends with a beatific vision of the Trinity bathed in Eternal Light.

Margaret Fleming

Paradise Lost

Paradise Lost is the great Christian epic which recounts the creation and fall of man. Although Milton uses many of the traditional epic conventions in relating the story he considered more significant than any yet commemorated in literature, he tries to better the classical models, not for his own glory, but for the glory of his subject.

Milton first, like Homer and Virgil, invokes his muse, this time the Christian Muse, who supposedly brought the law to Moses on Mt. Sinai:

> Sing, Heavenly Muse, that, on the secret top
> Of Oreb, or of Sinai, didst inspire
> That shepherd who first taught the chosen seed
> In the beginning how the heavens and earth
> Rose out of Chaos . . . (I: 6–9)

Other epic devices are a catalog of Satan's followers and a number of epic similes throughout the poem.

Most great epics contain major battle scenes, and this one is no exception. In Book VI Raphael describes in great detail the three-day war which took place in Heaven before the defeat and expulsion of Satan. Like the wars in previous epics, this one is divinely fought, with the outcome predetermined. God limits the strength of the angels so that Heaven will not be destroyed, and the fiends have the disadvantage of being able to experience pain but not death. Even though Satan invents the cannon, the sides are so evenly matched that God has to end the war by sending His Son to defeat Satan.

While the war itself demonstrates the futility of all violent conflict, the battle between the Son and Satan is fundamental to Christian theology because it foreshadows the ultimate victory of good over evil on earth as well as in Heaven. Milton emphasizes this conflict throughout the epic by contrasting his antagonists. In the first book Satan hypocritically volunteers to go to earth to corrupt man. Later, the Son selflessly volunteers to go to earth to save man from his corruption. Satan brings about man's downfall because of his envy and hatred; the Son brings man comfort because of his compassion. Finally Satan and his children Sin and Death bring man generations of misery, but Adam and Eve find hope in the fact that these years are leading to the Incarnation. Although Satan is victorious in the Garden, Milton makes it clear that he will not be victorious ultimately.

Unlike the heroes of preceding epics, the hero in *Paradise Lost* has control over his own destiny. Although God knows from the beginning what will happen in the Garden, He does not make it happen as do the gods in Greek and Roman epics. The responsibility for man's fate is man's because he was made "sufficient to have stood, though free to fall"; Adam falls by his own free choice.

Summary

The epic begins *in medias res* with Satan—formerly Lucifer, the angel of light—addressing his followers in the lake of fire. Evil has been created in his mind, and a great battle in Heaven has ended with his expulsion and theirs. Now, attempting to make himself appear heroic, the arch-fiend offers to find and corrupt God's newest creation, man, in an effort to regain Heaven. He deludes his fellow fiends into believing that his offer is sacrificial, but actually he wants to escape the torment of Hell.

In the meantime God and His Son, who have been discussing the new creation, observe Satan approaching Earth. With his foreknowledge, God explains to His Son that man will fall because of Satan's temptation and that someone will have to die to redeem him. When the Son offers to do this, there is rejoicing in Heaven. God's foreknowledge is not predestination, for man has free will and must freely choose salvation.

Having passed through the Limbo of Vanity, Satan, disguised as a heavenly being, now convinces Uriel, angel of the sun, that he has heard of man's beauty and wants to see it. Uriel gladly directs him to a mountain within the Garden of Eden, where he sees Adam and Eve. He is awestruck by their magnificence and their likeness to God, but still pursues his evil purpose. He appears to Eve in a dream, but while whispering in her ear he is discovered by angels and taken to Gabriel for questioning.

Next day the angel Raphael talks with Adam, telling him that he can become a spiritual being, but warning him that Satan has been found in the Garden. During the conversation he relates the events of the great war in Heaven. Adam then confides to Raphael the sensations of his first moments of awareness. He explains how he loves Eve and is fascinated with her beauty. Raphael warns Adam that he is the more rational of the two and should not allow himself to be overcome by Eve's charms.

The following morning Eve suggests that they work in separate areas in order to accomplish more. Adam strenuously resists because of the warning that Satan is in the Garden waiting to tempt them, but he eventually succumbs to Eve's charm, if not her logic, and they separate. The serpent appears to Eve and explains that she will be like a goddess if she eats of the forbidden fruit. She gives in to this appeal to her vanity and immediately becomes heady with what she believes is her new power. At first she hesitates to share her knowledge with Adam, but when she envisions him with another wife, she decides to offer him the fruit as well. Adam immediately realizes what has happened and is greatly saddened. He expects Eve to die at any moment, but because he does not want to live without her, he decides to share her mortality by eating the fruit. Now they both discover that they are naked and begin to quarrel and accuse each other of going against God's will.

As the communion between God and man is broken, the angels leave the Garden, but God comforts them with the assurance that they could not have prevented the Fall. When the Son comes to the Garden to administer God's justice, he is moved with compassion for the pair and clothes them. Learning of their impending destiny, Eve suggests that they kill themselves to prevent generations of suffering. However, Adam reminds her that their offspring will eventually bring about the Incarnation of the Son, and she is comforted.

Sin and Death, the children of Satan, build a road over Chaos and appear on earth to begin the destruction of mankind. Satan has returned to Hell, expecting a glorious reception from his colleagues, but to his surprise they curse him and become a mass of wriggling serpents.

The Son carries repentant prayers from Adam and Eve to the Father. He is moved with compassion but still sends the angel Michael to drive them from the Garden. Taking Adam to a hilltop, Michael shows him the panorama of all human history. The view is a bleak one, but Adam is comforted by the promise of Christ. Then Adam and Eve walk from the Garden, hand in hand, fallen but dignified, still in the image of God.

Carolyn Dirksen

References

Ciardi, John, trans. *Inferno,* by Dante Alighieri. New York: New
          American Library, 1964.
————. *Paradiso,* by Dante Alighieri. New York: New American
          Library, 1970.

Epics in America

Since Joel Barlow's *Columbiad* in 1782, an epic intent has been strong in American literature. Although the traditional form has undergone various modifications, American writers have continually tried to translate the heroic and nationalistic fervor of the Old World epics into New World terms. The most successful of these epic attempts are the following:

> *Song of Hiawatha,* by Henry Wadsworth Longfellow, 1855
> *John Brown's Body,* by Stephen Vincent Benét, 1928
> *Conquistador,* by Archibald MacLeish, 1932
> *Mountain Men,* by John G. Neihardt, 1915–1941
> *Paterson,* by William Carlos Williams, 1946–1958

Hart Crane's *The Bridge,* although epic in its conception, is of a different type, for it uses Brooklyn Bridge as a central metaphor for the entire poem, rather than a human protagonist. In all these works the conflict between cultures or moral codes, together with the impersonal and powerful forces of the land itself, provides the raw material for the epic design.

The form of the modern American epic is far more diverse and ambiguous than its Old World counterparts. While Longfellow, Benét, MacLeish, and Neihardt portray the physical struggles of their protagonists as vividly as do the ancient writers, Crane and Williams emphasize mental conflicts. Introspection becomes more important than the typical heroic virtues of courage and strength. The only constant seems to be the immensity and promise of the American continent as the backdrop for these two types of struggles.

The Song of Hiawatha

The American work that is probably most similar to Old World epics is *Hiawatha*. Longfellow uses the eight-syllable trochaic line of the Finnish *Kalevala* as well as a parallel setting and structure. Kaleva, the mythical land of abundance, becomes in *Hiawatha* the northern lake country of the North American continent; the *Kalevala*'s three brothers are incorporated into one central figure, Hiawatha, whose lineage is also both mortal and divine. The life passage of the hero and his accompanying growth in wisdom also follow the Finnish pattern. Invocations, catalogs, and alliterative repetition imitate other epic conventions.

Longfellow's most original accomplishment in this work is his skillful incorporation of Indian place names, proper names, and legend into the narrative. He was one of the earliest writers to recognize their poetic potential:

> From the land of the Ojibways
> From the land of the Dacotahs . . .
>
> Chetowaik, the plover, sang them,
> Mahng, the loon, the wild-goose, Wawa,
> The blue heron, the Shuh-shuh-gah . . . (p. 114)

The action of the poem moves toward Hiawatha's vision of a strong, united people, to be effected only when "springs the White-man's foot in Blossom," and when the land is full of people "speaking many tongues, yet feeling/But one heart-beat in their bosoms." Hiawatha's final departure "Westward! westward!" into the "fiery sunset" parallels the end of the *Kalevala;* his birchbark canoe, however, stamps this episode, like the rest of the poem, as undeniably American.

Lois Mervyn

John Brown's Body

This poem is perhaps the finest achievement of our two-century effort to create an American national epic. In his treatment of the Civil War, Benét integrates the experience of that conflict into a unified work that transcends both regional and social parochialism. He uses such epic conventions as invocations and catalogs, but, unlike the aristocratic heroes of older epics, Benét's Jack Ellyat is a democratic hero for readers with the democratic vision.

Structurally and thematically, John Brown is the center of the poem. He figures literally in the first book; then later he becomes the symbol for the entire antislavery movement. The action begins with his raid on Harper's Ferry and his subsequent hanging; its consequences are traced on various levels throughout the remainder of the poem.

The rhetoric of the larger figures—Lincoln, Davis, and the narrator—is balanced by concrete incidents in the lives of many minor characters, whose experiences often parallel one another. Thus the reader is kept aware of both the ideal and the actual throughout.

Rather than using a single poetic form, Benét gains dramatic contrast and intensity by shifting from one to another. He uses blank verse to describe the New Englanders:

> The mate went up on deck. The breeze was fresh.
> There were the stars, steady. He shook himself
> Like a dog coming out of water and felt better.
> (Prelude—The Slaver, p. 13)

The Southern gentry are portrayed in singing quatrains:

> So Wingate pondered in Wingate Hall
> And hated and loved in a single breath,
> As he tried to unriddle the doubtful scrawl
> Of war and courage and love and death. . . . (p. 66)

Benét also incorporates actual historical quotations in prose, such as John Brown's address to the Court:

> I have, may it please the Court, a few words to say. In the first place I deny everything but what I have all along admitted: of a design on my part to free slaves. . . . (p. 48)

This variety of expression represents many different persons and moods more successfully than a single form could have done.

The following portions of the poem are particularly dramatic and provocative:

> *Prelude—The Slaver:* a conversation between the captain and the mate which embodies the religious rationale for the transportation of the Negro.
> *Book I—John Brown's Prayer:* a fervent articulation of the religious exultation which played so important a part in the war.
> *Cudjo's Musings:* the devoted house servant views the gentry's shortcomings with amused detachment, but complete loyalty.
> *John Brown's Speech:* his actual address to the court, immediately prior to his execution.
> *Book II—Lincoln's Musings:* the misgivings and doubts which assailed the President.
> *Book III—Battle of Bull Run:* complacency turns to panic as the Congress and ladies watch this "picnic."

Book IV—Mary Lou Wingate: a lilting description of the duties of the lady of the Southern manor; a chilling recognition of her unflinching resignation to duty.

Book V—The Prisoners' Conversation: an amalgam of the bureaucratic dullness and the wretchedness of the prisoners, which characterizes all such situations.

Book VI—Invocation to the Song of Breath: a lyrical interlude with Whitmanesque overtones; a reminder of humanistic awareness at the nadir of human fortunes.

Book VII—Child Frightened by the Deserters: innocent childhood and hard-bitten soldiers.

John and Melora Vilas' Search: a poignant expression of the universal desire to step aside from unpleasantness, coupled with recognition of the inescapably powerful forces which embroil the girl and her father.

Jubilo!: an almost musical enunciation of the freed slave's thanksgiving.

Cudjo's Burying the Silver: the Southern hope symbolically buried.

Postlude: a final invocative summarization of the sacrifice and a plea for the future.

Lois Mervyn

Conquistador

This work was awarded the Pulitzer Prize for poetry in 1932. Though relatively short, it is an attempt to accommodate epic forms to New World experience. Its subject is Cortes' conquest of the Aztecs, as seen many years later through the eyes of his lieutenant, Bernal Diaz. This retrospective stance provides the reader with an old man's poignant double vision of past and present, as well as ironic insight into the expressed religious motivation for the conquest.

MacLeish begins his dedication with a quotation from Dante's *Inferno:* "O brothers, who through ten thousand perils have reached the west. . . ." He continues with a traditional poetic appeal to the dead, asking for their insight and true understanding of the past as an indication for the future. In these terms the entire conquest can be seen as the conventional epic descent into the underworld—another sort of Inferno.

The narrative embodies many other epic conventions: catalogs of armor, heroes, and treasure; accounts of bravery and treachery in battle; and exaltation of military valor. The narrator, however, adopts a determinedly unheroic posture, and Cortes himself is portrayed as consistently short-sighted and selfish.

The setting for the poem is painstakingly authentic. Mac-
Leish experienced the route "by foot and mule-back in the winter of
1929," and he proudly notes that his account "differs from that of
the historians." The Indian names, topographic descriptions, and
common names he uses will be particularly familiar to southwestern
readers.

Dante's influence is also seen in MacLeish's uses of varia-
tions on *terza rima.* The basic pattern is irregular anapestic triplets,
with occasional single lines or couplets for emphasis. The poet also
makes effective use of cross rhyme, resulting in a form of greater
complexity than at first appears:

> And our mouths were bitter with the bloody rheum:
> And we stood by the kettles and many were near death
> And our wounds cold and we talked of Montezuma: (p. 105)

Lois Mervyn

The Mountain Men

Largely because of failure in his poetic diction, Neihardt's
Cycle of the West—of which *Mountain Men* is the first volume—has
never been ranked among major American epics. Arthur Kay calls
him "a twentieth-century poet writing eighteenth-century verse upon
a nineteenth-century subject." But Kay also mentions his "genuine
epic temper," and reminds us that this poet wrote from personal
familiarity with his materials. This fact gives authenticity to his
accounts of the frontier figure. The work is worth reading, if only
for its stirring adventure and authoritative glimpse of our past.

Volume I is a trilogy. Book I, "The Song of the Three
Friends" (1919), traces the Ashley-Henry fur-trapping expedition of
1815 and recounts its exploits in the upper Missouri and Yellowstone
country. The protagonists are Talbeau, Carpenter, and the legendary
Mike Fink of the Davy Crockett adventures. A jealous quarrel over
an Indian woman and Fink's shooting of Carpenter violate the code
of camaraderie. As a result Talbeau becomes Fink's nemesis in an
agonizing revenge.

Book II, "The Song of Hugh Glass" (1915), also recounts
a betrayal of friendship and the true story of a wounded man's aston-
ishing endurance in the wilderness—the original Glass crawled some
one hundred miles after being abandoned by his companions. Although this section—the first written—has perhaps the weakest diction,
both the anguish and the unimaginable determination are caught in
Neihardt's account.

In Book III, "The Song of Jed Smith," written more than
twenty years later than Book I (1941), Neihardt shows not only im-

provement in poetic force but a real advance in narrative control. Instead of the cumbersome omniscient narration of the two earlier books, Neihardt here uses the personae of other mountain men to recount the story:

> "Yes," said Evans, "it was hell:
> But there was heaven too. I want to tell
> About the lives we lived, the deaths we died
> Together. I've been telling it inside
> These empty years alone." (pp. 57–58)

Probably the most remarkable of Neihardt's figures, Jed Smith is a spiritually and physically heroic man in the true epic tradition.

Volume II of the cycle includes "The Twilight of the Sioux," "Song of the Indian Wars," and "The Messiah," recounting the final abortive attempt by the Sioux to recapture their old medicine against the white man. This volume generally has the weaknesses without the strengths of Volume I.

These poems contain much material that might be used to stimulate further research. The locale, the indigenous speech and dialect patterns, the historical ramifications—all provide valuable starting points for the study of American culture.

Lois Mervyn

Paterson

Paterson, produced in five volumes from 1946 to 1958, won the National Book Award in 1949 in its unfinished state. Like other writers attempting an American epic, Williams draws his primary inspiration from the land itself.

In the traditional epic men move among physical and historical phenomena. An epic "translation," such as Crane's *The Bridge,* replaces the human element with the bridge itself as a metaphor. Williams' poem is an interesting combination of these two genres. The setting is realistic—the mountain and falls of the Passaic, where Paterson, New Jersey, is located. But the city, the physical locale, and the poet's alter ego, "Dr. Paterson," all merge into a single speaking consciousness. Williams illuminates the significance of this combination in his epigraph from Santayana:

> Cities are a second body for the human mind, a second organism, more rational, permanent, and decorative . . . ;
> a work of natural yet moral art, where the soul sets up her trophies. (p. 94)

Williams uses a variable foot, which relies on accentual rather than syllabic stress and seems to be particularly suitable for conveying nuances of American idiom:

> I asked him, What do you do?
>   He smiled patiently, The typical American question.
> In Europe they would ask, What are you doing? Or,
> What are you doing now?
>   What do I do? I listen, to the water falling.   (No
> sound of it here but with the wind!)   This is my entire
> occupation.   (p. 45)

The narrative also incorporates other forms, such as prose accounts taken from old Paterson newspapers and letters written by different characters. One series purports to be from a woman to Dr. Paterson, recounting the anguish and loneliness of the poet. Another group—from a young Negro to his mistress—betray his feeling of cultural shock. Excerpts from the letters of a modern shepherd—Corydon—reveal a would-be poet.

Like Eliot and Pound, Williams attempts to dramatize the entire contemporary milieu, but his work is more accessible, largely because his images depend on historical rather than literary allusion. His attitude toward life also seems more affirmative than theirs.

Paterson shows human experience—historical and emotional—against the backdrop of nature, which is altering man at the same time that man alters his surroundings:

> What end but love, that stares death in the eye?
> A city, a marriage—that stares death
> in the eye
> The riddle of a man and a woman . . . .
>   tho' love seems to beget
> only death in the old plays, only death, it is
> as tho' they wished death rather than to face
> infamy, the infamy of old cities. . . . (p. 106)

Paterson is a challenging attempt to answer questions about the nature of poetry, history, natural phenomena—and ourselves. It takes the American epic beyond traditional boundaries, proving that the genre is far from exhausted in its possibilities.

Lois Mervyn

References

Benét, Stephen Vincent. *John Brown's Body*. New York: Rinehart
    Co., 1928.
Kay, Arthur. *The Epic Intent and the American Dream*. Unpub-
    lished doctoral dissertation. Ann Arbor: University Micro-
    films, Mic., 61-2660.
Longfellow, Henry Wadsworth. *Complete Poetical Works of Henry
    Wadsworth Longfellow*. Boston: Houghton Mifflin Co.,
    1893.
MacLeish, Archibald. *Conquistador*. Boston: Houghton Mifflin Co.,
    1932.
Neihardt, John G. *The Mountain Men*. Lincoln: University of Ne-
    braska Press, 1953.
Williams, William Carlos. *Paterson*. Books 1-5. New York: New
    Directions, 1963.

Epic Themes and Techniques
Illustrated in Translations of the Iliad

The following seven passages from the *Iliad,* each presented in as many as eight different translations, were chosen to illustrate both epic themes and epic techniques. The passages are:

A. I. 1–7. The poet's invocation to the muse. It was conventional for epic poets to begin by asking for divine inspiration.

B. IX. 388–416. Achilles' refusal of Agamemnon's offer of reconciliation. This passage shows the social and material values of the Greeks. It also presents the idea of alternative fates: a short, glorious life, or a long and undistinguished one.

C. XIV. 493–500. Peneleos' killing of Ilioneus. This is a good example of Homer's vivid descriptions of violence and death. The seemingly incongruous poppy simile is typical of Homer's juxtaposition of war and nature.

D. XVII. 52–58. The simile of an olive tree. This beautiful description marks a brief idyllic pause between scenes of violence.

E. XVII. 425–426. The iron din of battle. Metaphors are comparatively rare in Homer. This is one of his most poetic.

F. XXIV. 49. Mankind's ability to endure suffering. This line is one that Matthew Arnold felt could be used as a touchstone because it is such a perfect fusion of idea and language. He translated it, "For an enduring heart have the destinies appointed to the children of men."

G. XXIV. 503–512. Priam's plea to Achilles to let him ransom Hector's body. This is the emotional climax of the *Iliad,* as Achilles is moved to compassion for the aged Priam and recognizes his own mortality.

Comparing several translations will help give the teacher some idea of what to look for when choosing a translation. The eight translations represented here do not constitute an exhaustive list (at least seven others are available in paperback editions alone), but each represents a different poetic or linguistic form. In addition, the first three are of historical interest. Any successful translation of Homer represents a blend of scholarship and poetry, and it is interesting to note that the first three and the last translation were done by practicing poets. The translators, in chronological order, are:

1. George Chapman. He published his famous translation, the first in English, over the period from 1598 to 1611. This is the Chapman's Homer that Keats first looked into. Chapman used a verse form called "fourteeners," from the number of syllables in each line. The poem consists of rhymed couplets, each line having 7 beats, usually in a 4–3 pattern.

2. Alexander Pope. His translation over a century later than Chapman's (1715–1720) —was widely acclaimed. Pope used heroic couplets—rhymed iambic pentameter. The couplet is usually a self-contained sentence, and balance and parallelism are noticeable features. Pope added quite a bit to Homer.

3. William Cullen Bryant. This translation, published in 1870, a century and a half later than Pope's, uses blank verse. It is quite faithful to the original.

4. Andrew Lang, Walter Leaf, and Ernest Myers. These three scholars collaborated on a prose translation, first published in 1882. Their version is very accurate, but the prose is archaic, suggesting Homer's antiquity.

5. William H. D. Rouse. This translation, also in prose, was first published in 1938. Rouse is as deliberately colloquial as Lang, Leaf, and Myers are archaic, but the colloquialisms are British, and the translation is now thirty-five years old, so it does sound a bit strange to modern American ears.

6. William Benjamin Smith and Walter Miller. This translation, published in 1944, is very literal, following the original line for line. Furthermore, it is done in dactylic hexameters, thus reproducing Homer's meter as closely as is possible in English. However, Homer's dactyl was quantitative, one long and two short syllables; in musical notation it could be represented by one half note and two quarter notes. The dactylic foot in English consists of one stressed and two unstressed syllables. This translation becomes sing-song after a while.

7. Richard Lattimore. This poetic translation, published

in 1951, uses a free six-beat line, unrhymed. The verse
form is unobtrusive, and it reads much more easily than
Smith and Miller's.
8. Robert Graves. This 1959 retelling, perhaps too free
to be called a translation, is basically informal prose
interspersed with verse translations of the more pro-
phetic and lyrical passages.

Comparing several translations can, for the student, partially compensate for not knowing the language of the original. By subtracting
anything that occurs in only one translation and comparing what is
the same in all, a reader can pretty well tell what the original must
have said. Furthermore, going over several versions of a key passage
is a subtle way of emphasizing its theme. These passages could also
be used in a study of the history of the English language, in both
vocabulary and sentence structure, or as a basis for comparing the
effects of differing sentence patterns and rhetorical styles.

A.   I. 1–7. The poet's invocation to the muse.

Achilles' baneful wrath resound, O Goddesse, that imposd
Infinite sorrowes on the Greekes, and many brave soules losd
From breasts Heroique—sent them farre, to that invisible cave
That no light comforts; and their lims to dogs and vultures gave.
To all which Jove's will gave effect; from whom first strife begunne
Betwixt Atrides, king of men, and Thetis' godlike Sonne.
                                        Chapman, p. 23

Achilles' wrath to Greece the direful spring
Of woes unnumber'd, heavenly goddess, sing!
The wrath which hurl'd to Pluto's gloomy reign
The souls of mighty chiefs untimely slain;
Whose limbs unburied on the naked shore,
Devouring dogs and hungry vultures tore:
Since great Achilles and Atrides strove,
Such was the sovereign doom, and such the will of Jove.
                                        Pope, pp. 25–26

O Goddess! sing the wrath of Peleus' son,
Achilles; sing the deadly wrath that brought
Woes numberless upon the Greeks, and swept
To Hades many a valiant soul, and gave
Their limbs a prey to dogs and birds of air,—
For so had Jove appointed,—from the time

When the two chiefs, Atrides, king of men,
And great Achilles, parted first as foes.
                                        Bryant I, p. 1

Sing, goddess, the wrath of Achilles Peleus' son, the ruinous
wrath that brought on the Achaians woes innumerable, and
hurled down into Hades many strong souls of heroes, and gave
their bodies to be a prey to dogs and all winged fowls; and so the
counsel of Zeus wrought out its accomplishment from the day
when first strife parted Atreides king of men and noble Achilles.
                                        Lang, Leaf, and Myers, p. 1

An angry man—there is my story: the bitter rancour of Achilles,
prince of the house of Peleus, which brought a thousand troubles
upon the Achaian host. Many a strong soul it sent down to
Hades, and left the heroes themselves a prey to dogs and carrion
birds, while the will of God moved on to fulfilment.
        It began first of all with a quarrel between my Lord
King Agamemnon of Atreus' line and the Prince Achilles.
                                        Rouse, p. 11

Sing, O Goddess, the wrath of Achilles, scion of Peleus,
Ruinous wrath, that afflicted with numberless woes the Achaeans,
Hurling headlong to Hades souls many and brave ones—of heroes
Slain—ay, gave unto dogs, unto all birds lonelily flying
Them as a prey; and the counsel of Zeus moved aye to fulfilment
E'en from the time when first stood parted in quarrel asunder
Atreus' son, the monarch of men, and godlike Achilles
                                        Smith and Miller, p. 1

Sing, goddess, the anger of Peleus' son Achilleus
and its devastation, which put pains thousandfold upon the
                Achaians,
hurled in their multitudes to the house of Hades strong souls
of heroes, but gave their bodies to be the delicate feasting
of dogs, of all birds, and the will of Zeus was accomplished
since that time when first there stood in division of conflict
Atreus' son the lord of men and brilliant Achilleus.
                                        Lattimore, p. 59

Sing, MOUNTAIN GODDESS, sing through me
That anger which most ruinously
Inflamed Achilles, Peleus' son,
And which, before the tale was done,
Had glutted Hell with champions—bold,

Stern spirits by the thousandfold;
Ravens and dogs their corpses ate.
For thus did ZEUS, who watched their fate,
See his resolve, first taken when
Proud Agamemnon, King of men,
An insult on Achilles cast,
Achieve accomplishment at last.

                                        Graves, p. 29

B. IX. 388–416. Achilles' refusal of Agamemnon's offer of reconciliation.

Atrides' daughter never shall be led
(An ill-match'd consort) to Achilles' bed;
Like golden Venus though she charm'd the heart,
And vied with Pallas in the works of art.
Some greater Greek let those high nuptials grace,
I hate alliance with a tyrant's race.
If Heaven restore me to my realms with life,
The reverend Peleus shall elect my wife.
Thessalian nymphs there are, of form divine,
And kings that sue to mix their blood with mine.
Bless'd in kind love, my years shall glide away,
Content with just hereditary sway;
There, deaf forever to the martial strife,
Enjoy the dear prerogative of life.
Life is not to be bought with heaps of gold;
Not all Apollo's Pythian treasures hold,
Or Troy once held, in peace and pride of sway,
Can bribe the poor possession of a day!
Lost herds and treasures we by arms regain,
And steeds unrivall'd on the dusty plain:
But from our lips the vital spirit fled,
Returns no more to wake the silent dead.
My fates long since by Thetis were disclosed,
And each alternate, life or fame, proposed;
Here if I stay, before the Trojan town,
Short is my date, but deathless my renown:
If I return, I quit immortal praise
For years on years, and long-extended days.

                                        Pope, p. 175

And the daughter of Agamemnon son of Atreus will I not wed,
not were she the rival of golden Aphrodite for fairness and for
handiwork matched bright-eyed Athene—not even then will I

wed her; let him choose him of the Achaians another that is his peer and is more royal than I. For if the gods indeed preserve me and I come unto my home, then will Peleus himself seek me a wife. Many Achaian maidens are there throughout Hellas and Phthia, daughters of princes that ward their cities; whomsoever of these I wish will I make my dear lady. Very often was my high soul moved to take me there a wedded wife, a help meet for me, and have joy of the possessions that the old man Peleus possesseth. For not of like worth with life hold I even all the wealth that men say was possessed of the well-peopled city of Ilios in days of peace gone by, before the sons of the Achaians came; neither all the treasure that the stone threshold of the archer Phoebus Apollo encompasseth in rocky Pytho. For kine and goodly flocks are to be had for the harrying, and tripods and chestnut horses for the purchasing; but to bring back man's life neither harrying nor earning availeth when once it hath passed the barrier of his lips. For thus my goddess mother telleth me, Thetis the silver-footed, that twain fates are bearing me to the issue of death. If I abide here and besiege the Trojans' city, then my returning home is taken from me, but my fame shall be imperishable; but if I go home to my dear native land, my high fame is taken from me, but my life shall endure long while, neither shall the issue of death soon reach me.

Lang, Leaf, and Myers,
pp. 172–173

His daughter! I will not marry a daughter of my lord King Agamemnon, not if her beauty challenged golden Aphrodite, not if her skill were a match for Athena Brighteyes. No, even so I will not do it! Let him choose her another man, one of his own rank who is a greater king than I. For if the gods let me live and return home, Peleus no doubt will find me a wife himself. There are women in plenty all over Hellas and Phthia, daughters of princes who have cities under their protection; I will take one of these to be my wife. When I was there, I often used to wish to marry a lawful wife, a mate well suited to me, and to enjoy the possessions which Peleus had gotten. For to me life is worth more than all the wealth of that noble city Ilios in peace time, before our armies came, more than the treasures in rocky Pytho within the doorstone of Phoibos Apollo the Archer. You may seize cattle and sheep, you may get tripods and horses, but for a man's life to come again neither seizing nor catching will help, when once it has passed beyond the fence of the teeth. My mother Thetis Silverfoot says, that two different fates are carrying me on the road to death. If

I stay here and fight before the city of Troy, there will be no
home-coming for me but my fame shall never die; if I go home
to my native land, there will be no great fame for me, but I
shall live long and not die an early death.

Rouse, pp. 109–110

'Tell him that I would not marry any daughter of his, not even
if she rivalled Aphrodite the Golden in beauty, and Athene the
Owl-Eyed in arts and crafts! Let him match them with bride-
grooms of his own rank, and of better blood than mine. . . If
the gods accept my sacrifice and bring us safely across the sea,
my father King Peleus will himself find me a wife. There are
enough girls in Phthia and the rest of Greece to pick from,
daughters of princes who rule fortified towns. While still at
home, I often considered marrying a loyal and capable wife
and settling down to enjoy my inheritance.

'And another thing: I value life far more than I covet
wealth—albeit such wealth as the Trojans amassed during the
years of peace, or Apollo the Archer has heaped in the massive
temple he raised at rocky Delphi. Herds and flocks may be won
in forays; tripods and chestnut horses may be peacefully bought;
but neither raiding nor trading can redeem a man's soul once
it has fled from his dying lips. My goddess-mother, Thetis the
Silver-Footed, prophesied as follows:

"Twin fates dispute your death, heroic son,
Of which two fates you must, perforce, choose one:
Either to stand fast on the Trojan shore
Until you die, renowned for evermore,
Or to retreat and from your Phthian town
Rule long, nor hope for any high renown."

Graves, p. 147

C. XIV. 493–500. Peneleos' killing of Ilioneus.

Full in his eye the weapon chanced to fall,
And from the fibres scoop'd the rooted ball,
Drove through the neck, and hurl'd him to the plain;
He lifts his miserable arms in vain!
Swift his broad falchion fierce Peneleus spread,
And from the spouting shoulders struck his head;
To earth at once the head and helmet fly;
The lance, yet sticking through the bleeding eye,
The victor seized; and as aloft he shook
The gory visage, thus insulting spoke:

Pope, pp. 269–270

Him did Peneleos wound beneath the brows, at the bases of the
eye, and drave out the eyeball, and the spear went clean through
the eye and through the nape of the neck, and he fell back,
stretching out both his hands. And Peneleos, drawing forth his
sharp sword, smote him on the middle of the neck, and smote
off even to the ground the head with the helmet, and still the
strong spear stood in the eye, and lifting it up like a poppy
head, he showed it to the Trojans, and spoke his boastful words:

Lang, Leaf, and Myers, p. 288

This man Peneleos caught underneath the brow, at the bases
of the eye, and pushed the eyeball out, and the spear went clean
        through
the eye-socket and tendon of the neck, so that he went down
backward, reaching out both hands, but Peneleos drawing
his sharp sword hewed at the neck in the middle, and so dashed
        downward
the head, with helm upon it, while still on the point of the big
        spear
the eyeball stuck. He, lifting it high like the head of a poppy,
displayed it to the Trojans and spoke vaunting over it:

Lattimore, p. 307

The spear shot down into Ilioneus' eye, gouging out the eyeball, and emerged at the nape. As Ilioneus flung open his arms,
Peneleos beheaded him. 'Trojans,' he cried, 'pray warn Phorbas
and his wife to mourn their loss; and when we sail home from
here, we will take the wife of Promachus a similar message!'
With that he lifted his spear. Ilioneus' head, impaled by the
blade, made it look like a tall poppy.

Graves, p. 217

D. XVII. 52–58. The simile of an olive tree.

And when alone in some choice place a husband-man hath set
The young plant of an Olive tree, whose roote being ever fed
With plentie of delicious springs, his branches bravely spred
And all his fresh and lovely head growne curld with snowy flowres
That dance and florish with the winds that are of gentlest powres;
But when a whirlewind (got aloft) stoopes with a sodaine gale,
Teares from his head his tender curles, and tosseth therewithall
His fixt roote from the hollow mines:

Chapman, pp. 349–350

As when some husbandman
Rears in a lonely and well-watered spot
An olive-tree with widely spreading boughs,
Beautiful with fresh shoots, and putting forth
White blossoms, gently waved by every wind,
A sudden blast descends with mighty sweep
And tears it from its bed, and lays it prone
Upon the earth,—
                                        Bryant III, pp. 161–162

Like as a man rears lusty a sapling, a shoot of an olive,
All in a lonesome place, where bubbles abundance of water,
Beautiful shoot, fair-growing, with all kinds of breezes upon it
Blowing, to sway it about: and it bursts into blossoms of whiteness;
All of a sudden there comes a blast of a terrible tempest,
Wrenches it out of its place, and lays it on earth low-leveled:
                                        Smith and Miller, p. 362

          As some
slip of an olive tree strong-growing that a man raises
in a lonely place, and drenched it with generous water, so that
it blossoms into beauty, and the blasts of winds from all quarters
tremble it, and it bursts into pale blossoming. But then
a wind suddenly in a great tempest descending upon it
wrenches it out of its stand and lays it at length on the ground . . .
                                        Lattimore, p. 355

E. XVII. 425–426. The iron din of battle.

And thus through all th'unfruitfull aire an iron sound ascended
Up to the golden firmament—
                                        Chapman, p. 359

Then clash their sounding arms; the clangours rise,
And shake the brazen conclave of the skies.
                                        Pope, p. 324

          The iron din
Rose through the waste air to the brazen heaven.
                                        Bryant III, p. 180

So they fought on, and the iron din went up through the high
desert air unto the brazen heaven.
                                        Lang, Leaf, and Myers, p. 355

... and so they fought, while the iron din resounded through the
unvintaged air to the brazen sky.
                                          Rouse, p. 210

So they were fighting on, and the uproar, clamourous, iron,
Unto the heaven of bronze went up through th'unharvested ether.
                                          Smith and Miller, pp. 374–375

        So they fought on, and the iron tumult
went up into the brazen sky through the barren bright air.
                                          Lattimore, p. 365

The iron clamour ascended through the upper air until it rang
against the brazen vault of Heaven.
                                          Graves, p. 258

F.   XXIV. 49. Mankind's ability to endure suffering.

        Fates have given to all that are true men
True manly patience . . .
                                          Chapman, p. 479

Fate gives the wound, and man is born to bear.
                                          Pope, p. 429

                        for fate
Bestows the power to suffer patiently.
                                          Bryant IV, p. 157

For an enduring soul have the Fates given unto men.
                                          Lang, Leaf, and Myers, p. 479

. . . for the Fates have given mankind a patient soul.
                                          Rouse, p. 283

Seeing the fates have implanted a heart of endurance in mortals.
                                          Smith and Miller, p. 510

for the Destinies put in mortal men the heart of endurance.
                                          Lattimore, p. 476

Many who suffer worse losses than the son of Peleus—a brother
or a son, for example—resolutely dry their tears after the funeral,
because the Fates have taught them courage in adversity.
                                          Graves, p. 336

G. XXIV. 503–512. Priam's plea to Achilles.

        "O revere
The gods, Achilles, and be merciful,
Calling to mind thy father! happier he
Than I; for I have borne what no man else
That dwells on earth could bear,—have laid my lips
Upon the hand of him who slew my son."
        He spake: Achilles sorrowfully thought
Of his own father. By the hand he took
The suppliant, and with gentle force removed
The old man from him. Both in memory
Of those they loved were weeping. The old king,
With many tears, and rolling in the dust
Before Achilles, mourned his gallant son.
Achilles sorrowed for his father's sake,
And then bewailed Patroclus, and the sound
Of lamentation filled the tent.
                       Bryant IV, pp. 181–182

"O Achilles, fear God, and pity me, remembering your own
father—but I am even more to be pitied—I have endured to do
what no other man in the world has ever done, to lift my hand
to the lips of the man who slew my son."
        As he said it, he lifted his hand to the face of Achilles,
and the heart of Achilles ached with anguish at the thought of
his father. He took the old man' hand, and pushed him gently
away. So the two thought of their dead and wept, one for his
Hector while he crouched before the feet of Achilles, and
Achilles for his own father and then for Patroclus.
                       Rouse, pp. 291–292

"Yea, have awe of the gods and compassion on me, O Achilles,
Mindful of thine own father; and even more piteous I am;
Braved have I that which never on earth braved a mortal before
        me,
Lifting my hand to the lips of the man who hath slain my
        children."
        Thus he, and stirred in him a yearning to weep for his
        father.
Touching the old man' hand, he pressed him away from him
        gently,
Both of them then in remembrance, the one for man-slaying
        Hector
Bitterly wept as he groveled before the feet of Achilles,

Who was bewailing his father anon, and, anon again changing,
Wept for Patroclus; and moaning arose through all of the house-
      hold.
Smith and Miller, p. 529

'Honour then the gods, Achilleus, and take pity on me
remembering your father, yet I am still more pitiful;
I have gone through what no other mortal on earth has gone
      through;
I put my lips to the hands of the man who has killed my children.'
    So he spoke, and stirred in the other a passion of grieving
for his own father. He took the old man's hand and pushed him
gently away, and the two remembered, as Priam sat huddled
at the feet of Achilleus and wept close for manslaughtering
      Hector
and Achilleus wept now for his own father, now again
for Patroklos. The sound of their mourning moved in the house.
Lattimore, p. 488

Sample Linguistic Analysis, Iliad, I. 1–7

      The following observations and speculations are only
a few of many that could be made, but they suggest possible areas
of investigation. The table which follows itemizes significant differences in diction and word order between the eight translations
of the opening lines of the *Iliad,* complete texts of which are found
on pages 68–70.

Spelling

      Only Chapman's spelling is slightly archaic. Notice
lims for *limbs* and the final *e*'s on *sorrowes, goddesse,* and *begunne.*
Pope's contraction *unnumber'd* is no longer in common usage, but
the rest of his spelling and that of all the others is standard modern
English. In Anglicizing the Greek names, Lang, Leaf, and Myers
use the spelling *Atreides,* and Lattimore uses *Achilleus.* Both these
spellings are closer to the original Greek than the more familiar
Latin forms *Atrides* and *Achilles.*

Changing Usage

      One aspect of the history of the English language is
illustrated by the abandonment of certain archaic words in favor
of more up-to-date terms. For example, *wrath* in the earlier transla-

Sample Linguistic Analysis

Chapman	Pope	Bryant	Lang, et al.	Rouse	Smith/Miller	Lattimore	Graves
Nouns							
wrath	wrath	wrath	wrath	(angry)	wrath	anger	anger
lims	limbs	limbs	bodies	*them*	heroes themselves	bodies	corpses
Proper Names							
—	—	Peleus' son	Peleus' son	prince of the house of Peleus	scion of Peleus	Peleus' son	Peleus' son
Atrides	Atrides	Atrides	Atreides	Agamemnon of Atreus' line	Atreus' son	Atreus' son	Agamemnon
Jove	Jove	Jove	Zeus	God	Zeus	Zeus	Zeus
that invisible cave that no light comforts	Pluto's gloomy reign	Hades	Hades	Hades	Hades	the house of Hades	Hell
Adjectives							
baneful	the direful spring	deadly	ruinous	bitter rancour	ruinous	its devastation	ruinously inflamed

Epithets

Thetis' godlike son	great Achilles	noble Achilles	great Achilles	the Prince Achilles	godlike Achilles	brilliant Achilleus	Achilles
king of men	—	king of men	king of men	My Lord King	the monarch of men	the lord of men	King of men

Verb Phrases

strife begunne betwixt	strove	strife parted	parted . . . as foes	quarrel between	stood parted in quarrel asunder	stood in division of conflict	an insult . . . cast

Diction and Word Order

infinite sorrowes	woes unnumber'd	woes innumerable	woes numberless	thousand troubles	numberless woes	pains thousandfold	. . . by the thousandfold

Word Order of the Four Key Words in the First Sentence

Achilles	Achilles	Sing	Goddesse	angry	Sing	Sing	Sing
wrath	wrath	goddess	sing	my	goddess	goddess	goddess
resound	goddess	wrath	wrath	story	wrath	anger	anger
Goddesse	sing	Achilles	Peleus' son	Achilles	Achilles	Achilleus	Achilles
DO—	DO—	V—	Apostrophe—	Adj—	V—	V—	V—
V—	Apostrophe—	Apostrophe—	V—	Appositive—	Apostrophe—	Apostrophe—	Apostrophe—
Apostrophe	V	DO	DO	OP	DO	DO	DO

tions is replaced by *anger* in the later ones; *baneful* and *direful* by *ruinous*. Where Chapman uses *betwixt,* Rouse uses *between*. The idea expressed earlier by *strife* or *foes* comes out later as *quarrel* or *conflict*. *Woes* gives way to *troubles* or *pains*.

Social and Cultural Implications

The specific word *limbs,* used in the earlier translations, is replaced in some later ones by *bodies* or *corpses,* thus conforming more closely to modern usage. The use of *limbs* reflects the way the Greeks usually focused on the part rather than on the whole, as we do. The perception of the world thus represented in the language can also be seen in the Greek art of Homer's period, where bodies are seen to be collections of parts rather than unified wholes. Another psycholinguistic difference, this one with philosophical overtones, occurs in the translations of both Rouse and Smith and Miller. They use *them* and *themselves,* translating the Greek literally. These words suggest that to the ancient Greeks the body was the person, and the soul was something else.

Achilles is variously described by the translators as *godlike, great, noble, the Prince,* and *brilliant*. Graves deletes the adjective altogether. Possibly these differences demonstrate a change over the centuries in the qualities considered admirable. *Godlike* today sounds presumptuous, incongruous with our conception of God. *Great* is still a perfectly good word, but seldom applied to a military leader. Both *noble* and *Prince* have aristocratic connotations that may be distasteful. *Brilliant* is perhaps just right for today, suggesting as it does both intellect and superior performance. But perhaps Graves is even closer by using no adjective at all, in keeping with the conventions of modern fiction, which tries to show rather than to tell. And of course it is congenial with our democratic practice of disregarding titles.

How many *sorrows,* or *woes,* or *pains,* did the Greeks endure? Too many to count, say five of the translators, using four synonyms to say so: *infinite, unnumber'd, numberless,* and *innumerable*. The last three are cognate, two from the English root *number,* with the English prefix and suffix *un-* and *-less;* and one from the Latin root *numer-,* with the Latin prefix and suffix *in-* and *-able* (*-abilis*). These slightly varying forms show the richness and flexibility of the English vocabulary. Ironically perhaps, the two Latinate forms *infinite* and *innumerable* would in today's usage be preferred to the Anglo-Saxon *numberless* and *unnumber'd*. But Rouse, Lattimore, and Graves translate the same word as *by the thousand* or *thousandfold*. Actually the Greek word *myrios* (from which our *myriad* is derived) means countless or infinite, except when used as a numeral, when it means 10,000. This suggests that for the ancient Greeks, 10,000 was a number so large as to be virtually uncountable.

In the previous examples we see how language reflects culture and also how often it poses a problem for the translator, who must attempt to express one culture in terms used by another.

Names

Since the use of names differs in different cultures, this area of translation has its peculiar problems. In many early societies a hero's identity was very sharply defined by who his father was. The Greek suffix *-des,* meaning *son of* or *descendant of,* is simply reproduced in English by our first four translators (*Atrides* for Agamemnon). Rouse is more explicit with *Agamemnon of Atreus' line,* while both Smith and Miller and Lattimore say *Atreus' son.* Obviously acquaintance with the classics has declined to the point that *Atrides* is no longer comprehensible. When Graves says just *Agamemnon,* he further implies that today a man's paternity is of no real importance.

For the names of the gods, Chapman, Pope, and Bryant all use the Latin form *Jove,* probably because these forms were more familiar in the Renaissance. All the others use the Greek *Zeus,* except Rouse, who uses *God.* This form, because of its Judeo-Christian connotations, seems incongruous in the classical context. The translations also make use of both the Latin and Greek names *Pluto* and *Hades* for the same god, as well as the Christian term *Hell.* Interestingly, not all of the translators are consistent with themselves. Pope uses the Latin names for both gods. Lang, Leaf, and Myers, Smith and Miller, and Lattimore all use the Greek names for both. But Bryant couples *Jove* with *Hades,* Rouse *God* with *Hades,* and Graves *Zeus* with *Hell.* Hell, like Hades, is now thought of as a place, but it too was originally the name of a goddess, Hel. Both words thus illustrate the etymological change known as transference. Chapman, in translating the concept, makes use not of a proper name, but of an interesting circumlocution to express, as Pope also does, the idea of darkness.

Word Order

In the phrase *infinite sorrowes,* half the translations invert the normal order, placing the adjective after the noun. Chronology seems not to make any difference here, but rather the demands of meter and rhythm.

The main clause of the first line is cast into four different arrangements, excluding that of Rouse, who adapts so freely that he entirely reshapes the sentence. (He also claims the story as his, giving no credit to the Muse.) *Achilles' wrath* (twice) or *the wrath/ anger of Achilles* (five times) is the direct object in every version but Rouse's. The verb *sing* is imperative, and the apostrophe to the goddess occurs in three positions, beginning, middle, and end. The most frequent word order, occurring four times, is *sing/goddess/ wrath/Achilles,* which sounds natural enough, although a corresponding request in contemporary usage would be more likely to follow the order Bryant uses: *goddess/sing/wrath/Achilles.* (*Mary, sing* us that *song* about *Jesse James.*) None of the English versions reproduces the order of the words in the original, which is *wrath/ sing/goddess/Achilles.* Since the most emphatic position in Greek is the beginning of the sentence, it is effective to start with *wrath,* the major theme of the epic.

Formal Considerations

A rigid verse form can sometimes force an archaic usage ("scion of Peleus"), padding ("that invisible cave that no light comforts," and "Pluto's gloomy reign"), redundancy ("stood parted in quarrel asunder"), or omission (Pope omits the title "king of men" for Agamemnon). In such cases the choice appears to be determined more by metrics than by semantics. Although a prose translation is likely to be more accurate semantically, it is probably less accurate poetically. And a translator is constantly faced with the question: is it better to be faithful or colloquial? Unfortunately, there is no easy answer. Translation is always a compromise.

Margaret Fleming

References

Bryant, William Cullen, trans. *The Iliad of Homer.* Boston: Houghton Mifflin Co., 1935.
Graves, Robert. *The Anger of Achilles.* New York: Pyramid Publications, 1959.
Lang, Andrew, Leaf, Walter, and Myers, Ernest, trans. *The Iliad of Homer.* London: Macmillan Ltd., 1922.
Lattimore, Richard, trans. *The Iliad of Homer.* Chicago: University of Chicago Press, 1951.
Nicoll, Allardyce, ed. *Chapman's Homer.* Vol. 1. New York: Pantheon Books, 1956.
Pope, Alexander, trans. *The Iliad of Homer.* New York: Hurst and Co., n.d.
Rouse, William H. D., trans. *The Iliad.* New York: New American Library, Mentor Books, 1938.
Smith, William Benjamin, and Miller, Walter. *The Iliad of Homer.* New York: Macmillan Co., 1944.

Suggested Projects for the Study of Epics

1. Read one of the epics from the list.
2. Explore one of the following aspects of the epic or of the time in which it was written:
   a. clothing,
   b. social customs,
   c. food and eating habits,
   d. education or training of heroes,
   e. music,
   f. the place of women,
   g. art,
   h. weapons,
   i. values or ideals,
   j. the relationship of men and gods (or God),
   k. the relationship of men and nature,
   l. symbolism—animals, numbers, color, etc.,
   m. foreshadowing—dreams, visions, prophecies, etc.
3. Write an analysis of the leading characters and trace the fatal flaw in each one.
4. Analyze the structure of the epic.
5. Identify the epic conventions used and explain their effects.
6. Analyze the role of settings in the epic.
7. Explore one of the following aspects of the language:
   a. compare two or more translations of the epic;
   b. collect vocabulary words that are based on this epic;
   c. analyze the use of personal names or place names;
   d. find any stories, sayings, or expressions that come from the epic;
   e. compare a translation with the original language (if you can read it).
8. Compare the philosophies of two different epics.
9. Compare the behavior of the hero with that of a modern hero.
10. Compare an incident in the epic with a similar modern situation.
11. Look up the mythology or legends of the epic. Compare these with other myths or legends you know.

12. Read some modern stories based on incidents or characters from the epic. Write summaries of them and compare them with the epic.
13. Write some lines or verses based on the form of the epic (or the form of the translation).
14. Write a modern epic.
15. Write and produce a play using the theme and plot of the epic.
16. Write a story about a character in the epic.
17. Find art forms other than literature that are based on the epic.
18. Make graphic illustrations of life at the time of the epic.
19. Make models or puppets that show the clothing and weapons of the time.
20. Organize a sports tournament with games and sports similar to those described in the epic.
21. Prepare a banquet using the foods and customs described in the epic.
22. Make up a board game based on the epic.
23. Make models of the buildings or fortifications or ships in the epic.
24. Draw a map of the journeys, campaigns, etc., mentioned in the epic.
25. Make a slide-tape presentation of one incident in the epic.
26. Make a collage based on the epic.
27. Get together with several other students and role-play one of the situations in the epic.
28. Get together with several other students, and each play the role of the hero of the epic he read in a panel discussion with an interviewer.
29. Make a comic strip based on the epic.
30. Prepare a lesson and present it to the class, using material you have found in exploring any of these suggestions.

                              Edna Webb

Works of Art, Literature, and Music Based on Epics

Works of Art

Gilgamesh

Cavallani, Dino, Illustrations for *Gilgamesh*
Eliot, Henry Ware, line drawings

The Iliad

Ingres, *Jupiter and Thetis,* painting, Aix-en-Provence Museum
Rubens, *The Judgment of Paris,* oil painting
Achilles Dragging the Body of Hector Past the Tomb of Patroclos,
        vase painting, early 5th century B.C., Metropolitan
        Museum of Art
Exikias, *Ajax and Achilles Playing Draughts,* jar, Vatican, Rome
Priam Approaching Achilles to Ransom the Body of Hector, vase
        painting, c. 480 B.C., Kunsthistoriches Museum, Vienna
Flaxman, John, *Thetis before Jupiter,* engraving from Flaxman's
        The Iliad of Homer
Zeus Enthroned, engraving, Museo Real Borbonico
Giorgio de Chirico, *Hector and Andromache,* pencil drawing, 1917,
        Museum of Modern Art

The Odyssey

Burne-Jones, Edward, *The Wine of Circe,* painting
Carracci, *Polyphemus,* easel picture
Dali, Salvador, *Return of Ulysses,* ink blots, brush and pen drawing
Odysseus and His Men Blinding the Drunken Polyphemus, vase paint-
        ing, mid-7th century B.C., Eleusis Museum
*Odysseus in the Land of the Dead Is Approached by the Shade of
        Elpenor,* vase painting, second half of the 5th century
        B.C., Museum of Fine Arts, Boston

Odysseus Slaying the Suitors, vase painting, c. 450 B.C., State Museum,
    Berlin
Odysseus, Tied to the Mast, Listens to the Song of the Sirens, vase
    painting, c. 475–450 B.C., British Museum
Ulysses in the Land of the Lestrigonians, fresco, Vatican Library
Odysseus as a Beggar Approaches Penelope, terracotta relief, c. 460
    B.C., Metropolitan Museum of Art, Fletcher Fund

The Aeneid

El Greco, *Laocoon* (with a view of Toledo in the background),
    painting, c. 1601–1606, S. H. Kress Collection, National
    Gallery of Art, Washington
Reynolds, Sir Joshua, (The Death of Dido), painting
Rubens, (The Death of Dido), painting
Turner, J. M. W., (a number involving Dido and Aeneas), paintings
Greek Warriors Pouring out of the Wooden Horse, vase painting,
    Bibliothèque Nationale, Paris
*Neoptolemus (Pyrrus) Killing the Child Astyanax and the Aged King
    Priam,* vase painting, c. 465 B.C., Museum of Fine Arts,
    Boston
Agesandros, Polydomus and Athenodorus, *Laocoon,* statue, Vatican
    Museum, Rome
Bernini, *Aeneas Fleeing Troy with Anchises and Ascanius,* marble
    statue, 1619, Borghese Gallery, Rome
The Trojan Horse from Pompeii, fresco, Museo Nazionale, Naples

Shah-Nameh

Persian miniature paintings; see *A King's Book of Kings,* ed. Welch,
    New York: Metropolitan Museum of Art, 1972.

Divine Comedy

Holiday, Henry, *Dante and Beatrice,* painting, Liverpool Gallery
Dore, Gustav, *Divine Comedy,* engravings
Blake, William, *Divine Comedy,* drawings

Kalevala

Gallen-Kallela, Aksel, *Lemminkainen's Mother at Tuonela River,*
    painting

Literary Works

The Iliad

Coleridge, Hartley, "Homer," sonnet
Keats, John, "On First Looking in to Chapman's Homer," sonnet
Keats, John, "To Homer," sonnet
Yeats, William Butler, "Leda and the Swan," sonnet
Arnold, Matthew, "Palladium," poem
Auden, W. H., "The Shield of Achilles," poem
de Columna, Guido, *Gest Historiale of the Destruction of Troy*, poem
Chaucer, Geoffrey, *Troilus and Criseyde*, narrative poem
Lydgate, John, *Troy Book*, poem
Muir, Edwin, "Ballad of Hector in Hades," poem
Rosetti, Dante Gabriel, "Troy Town," poem
Tennyson, Alfred Lord, "Ocnone," poem
Weis, Theodore, "The Ultimate Antientropy," poem
Dryden, John, *Troilus and Cressida*, play
Euripides, *Hecuba*, play
Euripides, *The Trojan Women*, play
Giradoux, Jean, *Tiger at the Gates* (La Guerre de Troi n'aura pas
	lieu), play
Racine, Jean Baptiste, *Andromache*, play
Shakespeare, William, *Troilus and Cressida*, play
Sallaska, Georgia, *Priam's Daughter*, novel

The Odyssey

Lang, Andrew, "The Odyssey," sonnet
Brooke, Rupert, *Menelaus and Helen*, poem
Daniel, Samuel, "Ulysses and the Sirens," poem
Graves, Robert, "Ulysses," poem
MacLeish, Archibald, "Calypso's Island," poem
Pound, Ezra, Cantos I and XX, poems
Rosetti, Dante Gabriel, "For 'The Wine of Circe' by Edward Burne-
	Jones," poem
Tennyson, Alfred Lord, "The Lotus-Eaters," poem
Tennyson, Alfred Lord, "Ulysses," poem
Erskine, John, *The Private Life of Helen of Troy*, novel; *Penelope's
	Man*, novel
Joyce, James, *Ulysses*, novel
Kazantzakis, Nikos, *The Odyssey: A Modern Sequel*, novel
Rodo-Canachi, C. P., *Forever Ulysses*, novel

The Aeneid

Chaucer, Geoffrey, "Dido," *Legend of Good Women,* poem
Lowell, Robert, "Falling Asleep over the *Aeneid,*" poem
Ovid, *Heriodes* (Dido), poem
Tate, Allen, "Aeneas at Washington," poem
Tennyson, Alfred Lord, "To Virgil," poem
Euripides, *The Trojan Women,* play
Marlowe, Christopher, *Tragedy of Dido, Queen of Carthage,* play
Metastasio, Pietro, *Didone Abbandonato,* 1724, play (set to music by
        about fifty composers)

Beowulf

Gardner, John, *Grendel,* story
Serrailier, Ian, *Beowulf, the Warrior,* story

Shah-Nameh

Arnold, Matthew, "Sohrab and Rustum," poem

Song of Roland

MacLeish, Archibald, "The Too-Late Born," poem

El Cid

Corneille, *Le Cid,* play

Nibelungenlied

Morris, William, *The Story of Sigurd, the Volsung,* verse rendition

Divine Comedy

Longfellow, H. W., "Divina Commedia," poem
Rosetti, Dante Gabriel, "Dante at Verona," poem

Orlando Furioso

Woolf, Virginia, *Orlando,* novel

Musical Works

The Iliad

Berlioz, *Les Troyens,* opera
Offenbach, *La Belle Hélène,* opera

The Odyssey

Berlioz, *Les Troyens,* opera
Gounod, *Ulysse,* incidental music for tragedy by Ponard
Offenbach, *La Belle Hélène,* opera
Strauss, Richard, *The Egyptian Helen,* opera

The Aeneid

Purcell, *Dido and Aeneas,* opera

Song of Roland

Gluck, *Roland,* opera

El Cid

Massenet, *Le Cid,* opera

Lay of Igor's Campaign

Borodin, *Prince Igor,* opera

Nibelungenlied

Wagner, *Götterdämmerung,* opera

Lusiads

Bizet, *Vasco da Gama,* descriptive symphony with chorus

Jerusalem Delivered

Liszt, *Tasso,* tone poem

Kalevala

Sibelius, Jean, *The Swan of Tuonela,* tone poem

American Epics

Copland, *Billy the Kid,* ballet; *Rodeo,* ballet

Bibliography

Epic Translations Available in Paperback

For each of the epics listed below, the same passage has been reproduced as it has been variously rendered into English in available paperback editions. We hope that this will give enough of the flavor of each to help teachers in making choices among editions. While the order in which each epic is considered reflects the order of this book, available paperback editions have been listed alphabetically according to translator rather than chronologically. For most of the works, additional bibliographical information concerning the presence of critical discussion, diagrams, glossary, illustrations, maps, and summaries is also given, but since not every translation was available to us in its most recent edition, some information is lacking. The prices given are those of the November 1973 edition of *Paperbound Books in Print* (New York: R. R. Bowker Company).

Our sincere thanks go to all the publishers who sent us complimentary copies of these works. It was their generosity that made possible the compilation of this catalog.

Gilgamesh

Mason, Herbert, trans. *Gilgamesh: A Verse Narrative.* New York: New American Library, 1972, $1.25. Critical information, glossary.

> Gilgamesh knew his friend was close to death.
> He tried to recollect aloud their life together
> That had been so brief, so empty of gestures
> They never felt they had to make. . . . (p. 40)

Iliad, I. 1–7

Butler, Samuel, trans. *Iliad.* Edited by Walter J. Miller and Harry Shefter. New York: Washington Square Press, 1970, $.60.

Critical information, glossary, illustrations, maps, summaries.

Sing, O Goddess, the anger of Achilles son of Peleus, that brought countless ills upon the Achaeans. Many a brave soul did it send hurrying down to Hades, and many a hero did it yield a prey to dogs and vultures, for so were the counsels of Zeus fulfilled from the day on which the son of Atreus, Agamemnon king of men, and great Achilles first fell out with one another. (p. 1)

Chase, Alston H., and Perry, William G., Jr., trans. *The Iliad*. New York: Bantam Books, 1972, $.75. Critical information, glossary.

Sing, O goddess, of the wrath of Peleus' son Achilles, the deadly wrath that brought upon the Achaeans countless woes and sent many mighty souls of heroes down to the house of Death and made their bodies prey for dogs and all the birds, as the will of Zeus was done, from the day when first the son of Atreus, king of men, and godlike Achilles parted in strife. (p. 35)

Lang, Andrew, et al., trans. *The Compact Homer: The Iliad*. (Abridged.) Woodbury, N.Y.: Barron's Educational Series, 1963, $.95. Critical information, illustrations.
———. *The Compact Homer: Iliad and Odyssey*. (Abridged.) Woodbury, N.Y.: Barron's Educational Series, 1963, $1.95. Critical information, illustrations.
———. *Iliad*. Bridgeport. Conn.: Airmont Publishing Co., $.60.
———. *Iliad*. New York: Modern Library, $.85. Critical information.

Sing, goddess, the wrath of Achilles, Peleus' son, the ruinous wrath that brought on the Achaians woes innumerable, and hurled down into Hades many strong souls of heroes, and gave their bodies to be a prey to dogs and all winged fowls; and so the counsel of Zeus wrought out its accomplishment from the day when first strife parted Atreides king of men and noble Achilles.

Lattimore, Richard, trans. *The Iliad of Homer*. Chicago: University of Chicago Press, Phoenix Books, 1961, $2.25. Critical information, glossary.

Sing, goddess, the anger of Peleus' son Achilleus
and its devastation, which put pains thousandfold upon
     the Achaians,

hurled in their multitudes to the house of Hades strong
    souls
of heroes, but gave their bodies to be the delicate feasting
of dogs, of all birds, and the will of Zeus was accomplished
since that time when first there stood in division of conflict
Atreus' son the lord of men and brilliant Achilleus. (p. 1)

Pope, Alexander, trans. *The Iliad of Homer.* Edited by Roben A.
    Brower and W. H. Bond. New York: Macmillan Co., Col-
    lier Books, $2.95.

Achilles' wrath to Greece the direful spring
Of woes unnumber'd, heavenly goddess, sing!
The wrath which hurl'd to Pluto's gloomy reign
The souls of mighty chiefs untimely slain;
Whose limbs unburied on the naked shore,
Devouring dogs and hungry vultures tore;
Since great Achilles and Atrides strove,
Such was the sovereign doom, and such the will of Jove.

Richards, Ivor A., trans. *The Iliad: A Shortened Version.* New York:
    W. W. Norton and Co., 1950, $1.25. Critical information.

Sing, goddess, the anger of Achilles, the anger which
caused so many sorrows to the Greeks. It sent to Hades
many souls of heroes and gave their bodies to be food of
dogs and birds. So the design of Zeus was worked out
from the time when, first, Agamemnon, king of men, and
great Achilles were parted in anger. (p. 33)

Rieu, Emil V., trans. *Iliad.* Baltimore: Penguin Books, 1973, $1.65.
    Critical information, glossary.

The Wrath of Achilles is my theme, that fatal wrath which,
in fulfilment of the will of Zeus, brought the Achaeans so
much suffering and sent the gallant souls of many noble-
men to Hades, leaving their bodies as carrion for the dogs
and passing birds. Let us begin, goddess of song, with the
angry parting that took place between Agamemnon King
of Men and the great Achilles son of Peleus. (p. 23)

Rouse, William H. D., trans. *Iliad.* New York: New American Li-
    brary, Mentor Books, 1966, $.75. Glossary.

An angry man—there is my story: the bitter rancour of
Achilles, prince of the house of Peleus, which brought a
thousand troubles upon the Achaian host. Many a strong
soul it sent down to Hades, and left the heroes themselves

a prey to dogs and carrion birds, while the will of God
moved on to fulfilment. (p. 11)

Odyssey, IX. 345–49

Butler, Samuel, trans. *Odyssey*. Edited by Walter J. Miller and Harry
　　　Shefter. New York: Washington Square Press, 1973,
　　　$.75. Critical information, glossary, illustrations, maps,
　　　summaries.

　　　So I went up to him with an ivy-wood bowl of deep red
　　　wine in my hands. "Look here, Cyclops," said I, "you
　　　have been eating a great deal of man's flesh, so take this
　　　and drink some wine, that you may see what kind of
　　　liquor we had on board my ship." (p. 94)

Cook, Albert, ed. and trans. *The Odyssey: A New Verse Translation*.
　　　New York: W. W. Norton and Co., 1974, $1.75. Critical
　　　information, glossary.

　　　Then I addressed the Cyclops, standing close to him,
　　　Holding in my hands an ivy bowl of black wine:
　　　"Here, Cyclops, drink wine, now you have eaten human
　　　　　flesh,
　　　So you may see what sort of wine this is that our ship
　　　　　contained." (p. 123)

Fitzgerald, Robert, trans. *The Odyssey*. Garden City, N.Y.: Double-
　　　day and Co., Anchor Books, 1963, $1.95. Critical informa-
　　　tion, illustrations.

　　　My moment was at hand, and I went forward
　　　holding an ivy bowl of my dark drink,
　　　looking up and saying:
　　　　　"Kyklops, try some wine.
　　　Here's liquor to wash down your scraps of men,
　　　Taste it, and see the kind of drink we carried
　　　under our planks." (p. 155)

Lang, Andrew, and Butcher, S. H., trans. *The Compact Homer: The
　　　Odyssey*. (Abridged.) Woodbury, N.Y.: Barron's Educa-
　　　tional Series, 1971, $.95. Critical information, glossary,
　　　illustrations.
　　——. *The Compact Homer: Iliad and Odyssey*. (Abridged.) Wood-
　　　bury, N.Y.: Barron's Educational Series, 1963, $1.95. Crit-
　　　ical information, illustrations.

———. *Odyssey*. Bridgeport, Conn.: Airmont Publishing Co., 1965,
$.60. Summaries.

———. *Odyssey*. New York: Modern Library, 1950, $.85.

> Then I stood by the Cyclops and spake to him, holding
> in my hands an ivy bowl of the dark wine:
> > "Cyclops, take and drink wine after thy feast
> of man's meat, that thou mayest know what manner of
> drink this was that our ship held."

Lattimore, Richard, trans. *The Odyssey of Homer*. New York: Harper and Row, Torchbooks, 1967, $1.95. Critical information, glossary.

> Then at last I, holding in my hands an ivy bowl
> full of the black wine, stood close to the Cyclops and spoke
> > out:
> "Here, Cyclops, have a drink of wine, now you have fed on
> human flesh, and see what kind of drink our ship carried
> inside her." (p. 146)

Palmer, George, trans. *Odyssey*. Edited by Howard N. Porter. New York: Bantam Books, 1962, $.75. Critical information, glossary, summaries.

> And now it was that drawing near the Cyclops I thus
> spoke, holding within my hands an ivy bowl filled with
> dark wine:
> > "Here Cyclops, drink some wine after your meal
> of human flesh, and see what sort of liquor our ship held."
> (p. 125)

Rieu, Emil V., trans. *Odyssey*. Baltimore: Penguin Books, 1964, $1.25. Critical information.

> Then came my chance. With an ivy-wood bowl of my dark
> wine in my hands, I went up to him and said:
> > "Here, Cyclops, have some wine to wash down
> that meal of human flesh, and find out for yourself what
> kind of vintage was stored away in our ship's hold."
> (p. 148)

Rouse, William H. D., trans. *Odyssey*. New York: New American Library, Mentor Books, 1950, $.75. Critical information, glossary.

> At this moment I came near to Goggle-eye, holding in my
> hand an ivy-wood cup full of the red wine, and I said:

"Cyclops, here, have a drink after that jolly meal of mans-mutton! I should like to show you what drink we had on board our ship." (p. 100)

Shaw, T. E., trans. *Odyssey*. New York: Oxford University Press, 1961, $1.95

Then I went up to the Giant with an ivy-cup of my dark wine in hand and invited him, saying, "Cyclops, come now and on top of your meal of man's flesh try this wine, to see how tasty a drink was hidden in our ship." (p. 129)

Aeneid, IV. 165–68

Conington, John, trans. *Aeneid*. Edited by Wendell Clausen. New York: Washington Square Press, 1965, $.60. Critical information.

Dido and the Trojan chief find themselves in the same cave. Earth, the mother of all, and Juno give the sign. Lightnings blaze, and the heaven flashes in sympathy with the bridal; and from mountaintops the nymphs give the nuptial shout. (p. 65)

Copley, Frank O., trans. *Aeneid*. Indianapolis: Bobbs-Merrill Co., 1965, $2.25. Critical information, glossary.

The prince of Troy and Dido both had come
to a cave. The bride's attendants, Earth and Juno,
gave signal: lightning and empyrean flamed
in witness; high in the hills Nymphs made their moan.
(p. 74)

Day-Lewis, C., trans. *Aeneid of Virgil*. Garden City, N.Y.: Double-day and Co., Anchor Books, 1952, $2.50.

Now Dido and the prince Aeneas found themselves
In the same cave. Primordial Earth and presiding Juno
Gave the signal. The firmament flickered with fire, a witness
Of wedding. Somewhere above, the Nymphs cried out in pleasure. (p. 86)

Dickinson, Patric, trans. *Aeneid*. New York: New American Library,
    Mentor Books, 1969, $.95. Critical information, glossary,
    maps, summaries.

    Dido, Aeneas, together alone found shelter
    In the same cave.
            The Gods, Primeval Earth,
    And Juno convenor of marriages give their signal;
    The lightning streaks; they couple; the skies shudder;
    The vault of heaven feels that mortal surge;
    The nymphs from their hilltops shriek the cry of Hymen.
          (p. 79)

Dryden, John, trans. *Aeneid*. Bridgeport, Conn.: Airmont Publishing
    Co., $.75.
————. *Aeneid of Virgil*. Edited by Robert Fitzgerald. New York:
    Macmillan Co., Collier Books, $2.45.

    The queen and prince, as Love or Fortune guides,
    One common cavern in her bosom hides.
    Then first the trembling earth the signal gave;
    And flashing fires enlighten all the cave:
    Hell from below, and Juno from above,
    And howling nymphs, were conscious to their love.

Guinagh, Kevin, trans. *Aeneid*. New York: Holt, Rinehart and Win-
    ston, 1970, $2.00. Critical information, glossary, summaries.

    Dido and the Trojan leader came to the same cave. Earth
    first and then Juno as bridal matron gave the sign to be-
    gin the rite; the lightning flashed and the heavens were
    witness to the marriage, while the nymphs wailed from
    the highest peak. (p. 88)

Humphries, Rolfe, trans. *Aeneid of Virgil*. New York: Charles Scrib-
    ner's Sons, 1951, $2.95. Critical information, glossary.

    To the same cave go Dido and Aeneas,
    Where Juno, as a bridesmaid, gives the signal,
    And mountain nymphs wail high their incantations. . . .
          (p. 92)

Knight, William F., trans. *Aeneid*. Baltimore: Penguin Books, 1964,
    $1.25. Critical information, glossary, maps.

    Dido and Troy's chieftain found their way to the same cav-
    ern. Primaeval Earth and Juno, Mistress of the Marriage,
    gave their sign. They sky connived at the union; the light-

ning flared; on their mountain-peak nymphs raised their cry. (p. 102)

Mackail, J. W., trans. *The Aeneid, Eclogues and Georgics.* New York: Modern Library, $1.25. Critical information.

Dido and the Trojan captain take covert in the same cavern. Primeval Earth and Juno the bridesmaid give the sign; fires flash out high in air, witnessing the union, and Nymphs cry aloud on the mountain-top. (p. 67)

Mandelbaum, Allen, trans. *Aeneid.* New York: Bantam Books, 1972, $1.65. Critical information, glossary.

Dido and the Trojan
chieftain have reached the same cave. Primal Earth
and Juno, queen of marriages, together
now give their signal: lightning fires flash,
the upper air is witness to their mating,
and from the highest hilltops shout the nymphs. (p. 86)

Mantinband, James H., trans. *Aeneid.* New York: Frederick Ungar Publishing Co., 1964, $2.75. Glossary.

Dido and Aeneas arrive in a cave together.
Earth and Juno, goddess of marriage, give the signal.
Lightning flashes from the sky to witness the union,
And nymphs scream from the mountain-tops in celebration. (p. 73)

Mahabharata, "The Fatal Dice"

Bhoothalingam, Mathuram, trans. *Sons of Pandu.* (Children's book.) Madras. Dolton Publications, 1966. Thompson, Conn.: InterCulture Associates, $2.60. Illustrations.

Draupadi refused to come into the assembly hall. When Duchasana insisted she ran towards Gandhari's apartments for protection. It was then that Duchasana seized her by the hair and dragged her into the great hall. (p. 49)

Choudhury, Bani Roy, trans. *The Prince of Dwarka.* (Children's book.) New Delhi: Hemkunt Press, 1970. Thompson, Conn.: InterCulture Associates, $3.00. Illustrations.

(The game had been played and Yudhisthir had lost.) (p. 46)

Dutta [Dutt], Romesh C., trans. *Mahabharata*. (Abridged.) Bombay:
    Jaico Publishing House, 1944. Thompson, Conn.: Inter-
    Culture Associates, $1.20. Critical information.
Dutt [Dutta], Romesh C., trans. *Ramayana and Mahabharata*.
    (Abridged.) New York: E. P. Dutton and Co., 1972,
    $1.95. Critical information.

> At his words her chaste heart sickens, and with wild
>   averted eye,
> Unto rooms where dwelt the women, Queen Draupadi
>   seeks to fly,
>
> Vainly sped the trembling princess in her fear and in
>   her shame,
> By her streaming wavy tresses fierce Duhsasan held the
>   dame!

Narasimhan, Chakravarthi, trans. *Mahabharata*. (Abridged.) New
    York: Columbia University Press, 1965, $3.95. Glossary.

> On hearing these words, the miserable Draupadi rose up
> in sorrow and, covering her pale face with her hands,
> she ran to the ladies' quarters in the palace of the old
> king. Thereupon Duhsasana ran after her in hot pur-
> suit, roaring in anger, and caught hold of her by her long
> blue wavy tresses. He roughly dragged the defenceless
> Draupadi by her hair to the hall, while she quivered
> pitiably like a plantain tree in a storm. (pp. 52–53)

Rajagopalachari, C., trans. *Mahabharata*. (Abridged.) Bombay:
    Bhavan's Book University, 1951. Thompson, Conn.: In-
    terCulture Associates, $1.25. Glossary.

> Panchali rose trembling, heart-stricken with sorrow
> and started to fly for refuge to the inner apartments of
> Dhritarashtra's queen. Duhsasana darted after her, caught
> her by her hair and dragged her to the assembly. (p. 92)

Rao, Shanta Rameshwar, trans. *The Children's Mahabharata*. (Chil-
    dren's book.) Calcutta: Orient Longmans Ltd., 1968.
    Thompson, Conn.: InterCulture Associates, $2.85. Critical
    information, illustrations.

> He went to the apartments of Draupadi, calling
> out to her in a mocking voice, and he followed her into the
> inner rooms where she fled from him. He caught her by
> her long dark hair, and dragged her out of the house, down

the steps and through the dust into his chariot. And he
brought her thus into the hall before Duryodhana and
forced her to her knees before him. (p. 177)

Ramayana, "The Return to Ayodhya"

Choudhury, Bani Roy, trans. *The Story of Ramayan*. (Children's
    book.) New Delhi: Hemkunt Press, 1970. Thompson,
    Conn.: InterCulture Associates, $3.00. Glossary, illustra-
    tions.

> A few days after the festivities were over, Dasrath,
accompanied by his sons and their brides, returned to his
capital. Ayodhya was like a garden in spring, so tastefully
was it decorated to welcome the newly married couples.
There was gaiety and rejoicing everywhere. The happy
queens lovingly embraced their sons and the brides as they
entered the palace. (p. 23)

Dutta [Dutt], Romesh C., trans. *Ramayana*. (Abridged.) Thompson,
    Conn.: InterCulture Associates, 1966, $1.20. Critical in-
    formation, summaries.
Dutt [Dutta], Romesh C., trans. *Ramayana and Mahabharata*.
    (Abridged.) New York: E. P. Dutton and Co., 1972,
    $1.95. Critical information, summaries.

> With his wedded sons and daughters and his guard in
>   bright array,
> To the famed and fair Ayodhya, Dasa-ratha held his way.

> And they reached the ancient city decked with banners
>   bright and brave,
> And the voice of drum and trumpet hailed the home-
>   returning brave.

Rajagopalachari, C., trans. *Ramayana*. (Abridged.) Bombay: Bhavan's
    Book University, 1973. Thompson, Conn.: InterCulture,
    $2.95. Critical information, glossary.

> King Dasaratha returned to Ayodhya, accompanied
by his retinue. On the way, there were bad omens and
anxious Dasaratha asked Vasishtha what they portended.
Vasishtha replied that there was no need to be alarmed,
for though the birds in the air indicated approaching
trouble, the animals on the land promised a happy con-
summation. (p. 45)

Beowulf, XXII. 2988–97

Alexander, Michael, trans. *Beowulf*. Baltimore: Penguin Books, 1973, $1.05. Critical information.

> After these words the Weather-Geats prince
> dived into the Mere—he did not care
> to wait for an answer—the waves closed over
> the daring man. It was a day's space almost
> before he could glimpse ground
> at the bottom. (p. 98)

Crossley-Holland, Kevin, trans. *Beowulf*. New York: Farrar, Straus and Giroux, Noonday Edition, 1968, $1.95. Critical information.

> After these words the leader of the Geats
> dived bravely from the bank,
> did not even wait for an answer; the water seething
> received the warrior. A full day elapsed
> before he could perceive the bottom of the lake. (p. 72)

Donaldson, E. Talbot, trans. *Beowulf: A New Translation*. New York: W. W. Norton and Co., 1966, $.95. Critical information.

> After these words the man of the Weather-Geats turned
> away boldly, would wait for no answer: the surging water
> took the warrior. Then was a part of a day before he
> might see the bottom's floor. (p. 26)

Hieatt, Constance B., trans. *Beowulf and Other Old English Poems*. New York: Odyssey Press, 1967, $1.25. Critical information.

> After these words, the leader of the Geats pressed on
> courageously—he did not wait for an answer. It was a
> good part of a day before he could see the bottom. (p. 53)

Morgan, Edwin, trans. *Beowulf: A Verse Translation into Modern English*. Berkeley: University of California Press, 1967, $.95. Critical information.

> After these words the man of the Geats
> Hastened off eagerly—by no means lingering
> For any rejoinder; the surging water
> Closed over the warrior.
> It was almost a day then
> Before he could make out the form of the lake-floor.
> (p. 41)

Pearson, Lucien Dean, trans. *Beowulf*. Edited by Roland C. Collins. Bloomington: Indiana University Press, 1965, $1.75. Critical information.

> Upon these words the prince of Weder-Geats made bold haste—he would not stay for answer; the water's swell received the battle-man. A good part of the day went by before he saw the bottom. (p. 79)

Raffel, Burton, trans. *Beowulf*. New York: New American Library, Mentor Books, 1963, $.75. Critical information.

> As his words ended
> He leaped into the lake, would not wait for anyone's
> Answer; the heaving water covered him
> Over. For hours he sank through the waves;
> At last he saw the mud of the bottom. (p. 70)

Rebsamen, Frederick, trans. *Beowulf Is My Name*. New York: Holt, Rinehart and Winston, 1971, $2.50. First-person retelling incorporates background information.

> I found the bottom of that awful mere, as is now well known. (p. 69)

Wright, David, trans. *Beowulf*. Baltimore: Penguin Books, 1957, $.95. Critical information, glossary.

> After this speech the Geat prince set off courageously without so much as waiting for an answer. The tumbling water swallowed him up. It was the best part of a day before he saw the bottom of the lake. (p. 62)

Song of Roland, CLXVII

Harrison, Robert, trans. *The Song of Roland*. New York: New American Library, Mentor Books, 1970, $.95. Critical information.

> Count Roland sees the archbishop on the ground:
> he sees the entrails bulging from his body.
> His brains are boiling out upon his forehead.
> Upon his chest, between the collarbones,
> he laid crosswise his beautiful white hands. (p. 137)

Luquiens, Frederick Bliss, trans. *The Song of Roland*. New York: Macmillan Company, 1952, $1.25. Critical information.

> And when Count Roland saw him lying there
> In death, the red blood flowing free from wounds
> Innumerable, he crossed his fair white hands. (p. 76)

Merwin, William S., trans. *The Song of Roland*. New York: Random House, Vintage Books, 1970, $1.65. Critical information.

> Count Roland sees the Archbishop on the ground and the bowels sagging out of his body and the brain oozing over his forehead.
> On the breast between the two collarbones, he crosses the white and shapely hands. (p. 63)

Moncrieff, C. K. Scott, trans. *The Song of Roland*. Ann Arbor: University of Michigan Press, Ann Arbor Paperbacks, 1966, $1.65. Critical information.

> The count Roland sees the Archbishop lie dead,
> Sees the bowels out of the body shed,
> And sees the brains that surge from his forehead;
> Between his two arm-pits, upon his breast,
> Crossways he folds those hands so white and fair. (p. 73)

Sayers, Dorothy L., trans. *The Song of Roland*. Baltimore: Penguin Books, 1957, $1.25. Critical information.

> The Count Roland sees the Archbishop lie;
> He sees his bowels gush forth out of his side
> And on this brow the brain laid bare to sight.
> Midst of his breast where the key-bones divide,
> Crosswise he lays his comely hand and white. (p. 120)

Terry, Patricia, trans. *The Song of Roland*. Indianapolis: Bobbs-Merrill Co., 1965, $1.75. Critical information.

> Roland sees Turpin lying there on the ground,
> Entrails protruding from his enormous wounds;
> Above his forehead his brains are bubbling out.
> On Turpin's chest, between his collarbones,
> Roland has crossed the beautiful white hands. (p. 85)

Poem of the Cid, CXXVIII

Arnaud, Leonard E., *Poem of the Cid, Selections*. Woodbury, N.Y.: Barron's Educational Series, 1953, $.95. Critical information, summaries linking selections.

> The girls fainted, so strong were the blows.
> Blood spotted the skirts and bodices.
> The infantes of Carrion grew tired of whipping,
> Trying to see which of them whipped the better.
> Doña Elvira and Doña Sol could no longer speak.
> Both lay unconscious in the oak grove of Corpes. (p. 21)

Merwin, William S., trans. *Poem of the Cid*. (Bilingual.) New York: New American Library, Mentor Books, 1959, $.95. Critical information.

> They beat them so cruelly   they left them senseless;
> the shirts and the silk skirts   were covered with blood.
> They beat them   until their arms were tired,
> each of them trying   to strike harder than the other.
> Doña Elvira and Doña Sol   could no longer speak,
> they left them for dead   in the oak wood of Corpes.
>   (p. 180)

Simpson, Lesley Byrd., trans. *Poem of the Cid*. Berkeley: University of California Press, 1970, $1.95. Critical information, glossary.

> The princes whip them till they fall senseless, their garments soaked in blood. Each strives to outdo the other and they cease only when they can strike no more. Doña Elvira and Doña Sol are silent now and are left for dead there in the oaken woods of Corpes. (p. 105)

The Lay of Igor's Campaign, XIV

Nabokov, Vladimir, trans. *Song of Igor's Campaign*. New York: Random House, Vintage Books, 1960, $1.95. Critical information, glossary, diagrams, summaries.

> No chattering magpies are these; on Igor's trail Gzak and Konchak come riding. (p. 69)

Zenkovsky, Serge A., ed. "Lay of Igor's Campaign," in *Medieval Russia's Epics, Chronicles, and Tales.* New York: E. P. Dutton and Co., 1963, $2.95. Critical information, illustrations.

> It is not the magpies which have begun croaking,
> it is Khans Gza and Konchak
> who search for Igor's path. (p. 159)

Song of the Nibelungs, XIV. 998

Hatto, Arthur Thomas, trans. *The Nibelungenlied.* Baltimore: Penguin Books, 1965, $1.95. Critical information.

> The flowers everywhere were drenched with blood. Siegfried was at grips with Death, yet not for long, since Death's sword ever was too sharp. (p. 132)

Ryder, Frank G., trans. *The Song of the Nibelungs.* Detroit: Wayne State University Press, 1962, $4.95. Critical information.

> The flowers all around were wet with blood.
> He fought with death but not for long—what good?
> Death has always owned the sharper sword. (p. 200)

Divine Comedy, Inferno, XVII. 112–17

Bergin, Thomas G., ed. and trans. *Divine Comedy.* New York: AHM Publications, $1.45.

>   Here we made our way
> And peering down we saw souls deep submerged
> In filthy dung, as human privies yield.
> Throwing my glance yet deeper I could see
> A head so dark beshitten as to hide
> If he were clerk or layman.

Biancolli, Louis, trans. *Divine Comedy: Hell, Purgatory, Paradise.* New York: Washington Square Press, 1968, $1.45. Illustrations.

> We climbed up to it and looked down below
> Into a pit where people were immersed in dung
> That seemed to come from all the world's latrines.
> And while my eyes were scouring below,
> I saw one with his head so smeared with shit,
> I could not tell if he were priest or layman.

Binyon, Laurence, trans. *Portable Dante*. Rev. ed. Edited by Paolo
    Milano. New York: Viking Press, $2.95. Critical infor-
    mation. Includes *La Vita Nuova,* poetry, and prose works.

> Thereon we stood, and in the hollow showed
>   Down there a people dipt in excrement
>   As if from human privies it had flowed.
> And while I searched them with my eyes intent,
>   A head, whether clerk's or layman's none could
>   tell,
>   I saw, with ordure is was so besprent. (pp. 98–99)

Carlyle, John A., et al., trans. *Divine Comedy*. New York: Modern
    Library, 1950, $1.25. Critical information, diagrams.

> We got upon it; and thence in the ditch beneath,
> I saw a people dipped in excrement, that seemed as it had
> flowed from human privies.
>   And whilst I was searching with my eyes, down
> amongst it, I beheld one with a head so smeared in filth,
> that it did not appear whether he was layman or clerk.
> (p. 100)

Ciardi, John, trans. *Inferno*. New York: New American Library,
    1964, $1.50.
————. *Purgatorio*. New York: New American Library, 1961, $1.50.
————. *Paradiso*. New York: New American Library, 1970, $1.50.
    Critical information, diagrams in all.

> Once there, I peered down; and I saw long lines
>   of people in a river of excrement
>   that seemed the overflow of the world's latrines.
> I saw among the felons of that pit
>   one wraith who might or might not have been
>   tonsured—
>   one could not tell, he was so smeared with shit.
>   (p. 161)

Huse, H. R., trans. *Divine Comedy*. New York: Holt, Rinehart and
    Winston, 1964, $2.50. Diagrams, summaries.

> We reached that place, and down in the ditch
>   I saw people plunged in excrement
>   which seemed to have come from human privies.
> And while I was searching down there with my eyes,
>   I saw one with his head so smeared with filth
>   that you could not tell if he were a layman or a
>   clerk. (p. 90)

Musa, Mark, trans. *Dante's Inferno.* Bloomington: Indiana University Press, 1971, $2.95. Critical information, illustrations, summaries.

> there we were, and from where I stood I saw
> souls in the ditch plunged into excrement
> that might well have been flushed from our
> latrines;
>
> my eyes were searching hard along the bottom,
> and I saw somebody's head so smirched with shit
> you could not tell if he were priest or layman.
> (p. 150)

Sayers, Dorothy L., trans. *Divine Comedy.* 3 vols. Vol. 1, *Inferno* (Hell) ; vol. 2, *Purgatorio* (Purgatory) ; vol. 3, *Paradiso* (Paradise). Baltimore: Penguin Books, 1948, $1.65 each. Critical information, diagrams, glossary, summaries.

> Thence peering down, we saw people in the lake's
> Foul bottom, plunged in dung, the which appeared
> Like human ordure running from a jakes.
>
> Searching its depths, I there made out a smeared
> Head—whether clerk or lay was hard to tell,
> It was so thickly plastered with the merd. (p. 184)

Sinclair, John D., trans. *Divine Comedy.* Rev. ed. 3 vols. Vol. 1, *Inferno;* vol. 2, *Purgatorio;* vol. 3, *Paradiso.* New York: Oxford University Press, 1961, $2.95 each. Critical information, summaries.

> We went there, and thence in the moat below I saw people plunged in a filth which seemed to have come from human privies, and searching down there with my eyes I saw one with his head so befouled with ordure that it did not appear whether he was layman or cleric. (p. 233)

Orlando Furioso, VII. 80

Harington, John, trans. *Ariosto's Orlando Furioso: Selections from John Harington's Translation.* Edited by Rudolf Gottfried. Bloomington: Indiana University Press, 1969, $2.95. Critical information, glossary.

> Such men of arms as watched at the gate
> He slew; the rest he suddenly assailed;

Good was his hap that scaped with broken pate;
They took their heels whenas their hearts them failed.
Alcina now had notice all too late;
Rogero was so far it nought availed.—
But in another book shall be contained
How him Dame Logistilla entertained. (p. 169)

Hodgens, Richard, trans. *Orlando Furioso: The Ring of Angelica.*
(First part only.)   New York: Ballantine Books, 1973,
$1.25. Summaries.

Pretending to be going out to play, he rode out
of the ancient whore's lascivious palace and approached the
gate beyond which lay the road to Logistilla the good.
There were guards. He attacked them suddenly, riding
through them with sword in hand. He left some wounded,
some killed, then went right on, across the bridge. Before
Alcina had the news, Ruggiero was pretty far away. In
the next chapter, I will tell you what way he took, then
how he came to Logistilla. (pp. 108 09)

Rose, William Stewart, trans. *Orlando Furioso.* Edited by Stewart A.
Baker and A. Bartlett Giamatti. Indianapolis: Bobbs-
Merrill Co., 1968, $4.75. Critical information.

Assaulting suddenly the guardian crew,
He, sword in hand, the squadron set upon;
This one he wounded, and that other slew,
And, point by point made good, the drawbridge won:
And ere of his escape Alcina knew,
The gentle youth was far away and gone.
My next shall tell his route, and how he gained
At last the realm where Logistilla reigned. (p. 62)

Lusiads, VII

Atkinson, W. C., trans. *Lusiads.* Baltimore: Penguin Books, 1973,
$2.25. Critical information, maps.

Consider the Germans, that far-flung and head-
strong people who are even now in revolt against the
successor of St. Peter and have set themselves up a new
shepherd and a new creed. And, not content with the
blindness of their ways, they are engaged in unworthy
strife, not against the overbearing Turk, but against the
Emperor, whose yoke they seek to throw off. (p. 161)

Jerusalem Delivered, I. 1

Fairfax, Edward, trans. *Jerusalem Delivered*. New York: G. P. Putnam's Sons, 1963, $2.95. Critical information, glossary,
summaries.

> The sacred armies and the godly knight
>   That the great sepulchre of Christ did free
> I sing; much wrought his valor and foresight,
>   And in that glorious war much suffer'd he:
> In vain 'gainst him did hell oppose her might.
>   In vain the Turks and Morians armed be;
> His soldiers wild, to brawls and mutines prest,
> Reduced he to peace; so heaven him blest. (p. 2)

Epics in English Available in Paperback

These epics, written originally in English, are available in
the following paperback editions.

Faerie Queene

Spenser, Edmund. *Edmund Spenser: A Selection of His Works*. Edited
by I. C. Sowton. New York: Odyssey Press, $1.80.
————. *Edmund Spenser's Poetry*. Edited by Hugh Maclean. New
York: W. W. Norton and Co., $3.25. Annotated.
————. *Faerie Queene: Books 1 and 2, The Mutability Cantos, and
Representative Minor Poems*. Edited by Robert L. Kellogg
and Oliver L. Steele. New York: Odyssey Press, $2.15.
————. *Poetical Works*. Edited by J. C. Smith and Ernest De Selin-
court. New York: Oxford University Press, $4.95.
————. *Selected Poetry*. Edited by Leo Kirschbaum. New York:
Holt, Rinehart and Winston, $2.50.
————. *Selected Poetry of Spenser*. Edited by A. C. Hamilton.
New York: New American Library, Signet Books, $1.25.
————. *Selections from the Poetical Works of Edmund Spenser*.
Edited by S. K. Heninger, Jr. Boston: Houghton Mifflin,
$5.15.

Paradise Lost

Milton, John. *Complete English Poems of John Milton*. Edited by
John D. Jump. New York: Washington Square Press, $.90.
————. *Complete Poetry and Selected Prose*. Edited by Cleanth
Brooks. New York: Modern Library, $1.45.

———. *Complete Poetry of John Milton.* Edited by John T. Shaw-cross. New York: Doubleday and Co., Anchor Books, $4.95.

———. *Paradise Lost.* Edited by William G. Madsen. New York: Modern Library, $1.25.

———. *Paradise Lost.* Introduction by H. Bloom. Bound with *Paradise Regained, Samson Agonistes.* New York: Macmillan Co., Collier Books, $.95.

———. *Paradise Lost.* New ed. Introduction by F. Tromley. Bound with *Paradise Regained.* Bridgeport, Conn.: Airmont Publishing Co., $.95.

———. *Paradise Lost, a New Edition.* Edited by Merritt Y. Hughes. New York: Odyssey Press, $1.45.

———. *Paradise Lost and Other Poems.* Introduction by E. Le Comte. New York: New American Library, Mentor Books, $.95.

———. *Paradise Lost and Paradise Regained.* Edited by Christopher Ricks. New York: New American Library, Signet Books, $1.95.

———. *Paradise Lost and Selected Poetry and Prose.* Edited by Norton Frye. New York: Holt, Rinehart and Winston, $3.00.

———. *Paradise Lost: Poems.* Introduction by Richard Eberhart. Bound with *Paradise Regained, Samson Agonistes.* New York: Doubleday and Co., $5.95.

———. *Portable Milton.* Edited by Douglas Bush. New York: Viking Press, $2.95.

Hiawatha

Longfellow, Henry Wadsworth. *Evangeline and Other Poems.* Introduction by C. L. Bennet. Bridgeport, Conn.: Airmont Publishing Co., $.60.

———. *Evangeline and Selected Tales and Poems.* Edited by Horace Gregory. New York: New American Library, Signet Books, $.75.

———. *Poems.* New York: E. P. Dutton and Co., $2.25.

Conquistador

MacLeish, Archibald. *Collected Poems of Archibald MacLeish.* Boston: Houghton Mifflin Co., 1963, $3.75.

Mountain Men

Neihardt, John G. *Mountain Men*. Lincoln: University of Nebraska
    Press, $2.75

Paterson

Williams, William Carlos. *Paterson*. Books 1–5. New York: New
    Directions, 1963, $1.95.

Epics Available in Hardback Editions Only

Complete translations and/or editions of these epics are
available in hardback editions only.

Mahabharata

Chandra, Roy P., trans. *Mahabharata*. 13 vols. Columbia, Mo.: South
    Asia Books, 1972, $10 each.
Lal, P., trans. *Mahabharata*. 50 vols. New York: International Pub-
    lication Service, 1968–73, $225, set.
Van Buitenen, J. A., ed. and trans. *Mahabharata*. Vol. 1. Chicago:
    University of Chicago Press, 1973, $15. Additional vol-
    umes forthcoming.

Ramayana

Griffith, Ralph T., trans. *The Ramayana of Valmiki*. 3rd ed. New
    York: International Publications Service, 1963, $9.00.
Menen, Aubrey, trans. *Ramayana: As Told by Aubrey Menen*. New
    York: Charles Scribner's Sons, 1954, out of print. Re-
    printed by Greenwood Press, Westport, Conn., $11.75.

Shah-Nameh

Atkinson, James, trans. *Shah-Nameh*. By Abdul Kasim Firdausi.
    London and New York: Frederick Warne and Co., 1886,
    out of print. Prose and verse.
————. *Suhrab and Rustam: A Poem from the Shah Namah of
    Firdausi*. English and Persian. Reprint of the 1814 edition.
    Delmar, N.Y.: Scholar's Facsimiles and Reprints, 1972,
    $7.50.

Kalevala

Johnson, Aili Kohlemainen, trans. *Kalevala*. By Elias Lönnrot. Hancock, Mich.: The Book Concern, 1950, out of print. Prose.
Kirby, W. F., trans. *Kalevala*. By Elias Lönnrot. 2 vols. New York: E. P. Dutton and Co., Everyman Edition, $3.50 each.
Magoun, Francis P., Jr., trans. *Kalevala: Poems of the Kaleva District*. By Elias Lönnrot. Cambridge: Harvard University Press, 1963, $12.50. Illustrated.

John Brown's Body

Benét, Stephen Vincent. *John Brown's Body*. 2nd ed. New York: Holt, Rinehart and Winston, $4.12.
————. *John Brown's Body*. Annotated ed. Edited by J. L. Capps and C. R. Kemble. New York: Holt, Rinehart and Winston, 1969, $4.50.

Reference Works

General

Hamilton, Edith. *Mythology*. New York: New American Library, Mentor Books, 1940. Brief stories of the Greek, Roman, and Norse gods. Can be read by students.
Hornstein, Lillian, et al., eds. *The Reader's Companion to World Literature*. Rev. ed. New York: New American Library, 1973. Short articles, arranged alphabetically, on authors, works, and literary terms. Includes all the major epics. Concise and very helpful.
Leeming, David Adams. *Mythology: The Voyage of the Hero*. Philadelphia: J. B. Lippincott Co., 1973. Divides the voyage into eight stages: conception and birth, childhood, preparation and withdrawal, quest, death, descent to the underworld, resurrection, and apotheosis. Gives a number of stories from widely different cultural traditions as illustrations of each stage.

Ancient Epics

Beye, Charles Rowan. *The Iliad, the Odyssey, and the Epic Tradition*. Gloucester, Mass.: Peter Smith, 1966. Very clear explanations of oral composition, epic technique, and the world of the epic, as well as full discussions of the *Iliad,* the *Odyssey,* and the *Aeneid.*

Graves, Robert. *The Greek Myths: I.* Baltimore: Pelican Books, 1955. Brief retelling of myths, with discussions of their significance and comparison with similar myths in other cultures.

Hooke, S. H. *Middle Eastern Mythology.* Baltimore: Pelican Books, 1963. Discussions of myths from several cultures. Useful background for *Gilgamesh* and for Biblical stories as well.

Lord, Albert B. *The Singer of Tales.* New York: Atheneum Publishers, 1965. Explains the theory of oral composition. Based on studies of epic singers still alive today in remote parts of Europe.

Mayerson, Philip. *Classical Mythology in Literature, Art, and Music.* Lexington, Mass.: Xerox College Publishing, 1971. Excellent summaries of the myths and all other Trojan War material, as well as discussion of the various art works based on them.

Reinhold, Meyer. *Greek and Roman Classics.* Woodbury, N.Y.: Barron's Educational Series, 1946. Clear outlines and summaries of major works, including the *Iliad,* the *Odyssey,* and the *Aeneid.*

Zimmerman, J. E. *Dictionary of Classical Mythology.* New York: Bantam Books, 1964. Tells a little about each name, also how to pronounce it.

Medieval Epics

Ellis-Davidson, H. R. *Gods and Myths of Northern Europe.* Baltimore: Pelican Books, 1964. Retelling and discussion of the Norse and Icelandic myths. Good background for the Icelandic sagas, the *Nibelungenlied,* and *Beowulf.*

Mirsky, D. M. *A History of Russian Literature.* New York: Random House, Vintage Books, 1958. Useful for study of the *Lay of Igor's Campaign.*

Renaissance Epics

Brand, C. P. *Torquato Tasso: A Study of the Poet and of His Contribution to English Literature.* New York: Cambridge University Press, 1965.

Durling, Robert M. *The Figure of the Poet in Renaissance Epic.* Cambridge: Harvard University Press, 1965.

Giamatti, A. Bartlett. *The Earthly Paradise and the Renaissance Epic.* Princeton: Princeton University Press, 1966.
Pierce, Frank, ed. *Luis De Camoes: Os Lusiadas.* New York: Oxford University Press, 1973. Introduction is in English.
Rich, Townsend. *Harington and Ariosto.* New Haven: Yale University Press, 1940.
Tillyard, Eustace M. W. *The English Epic and Its Background.* New York: Oxford University Press, 1954.

American Epics

Bradley, Sculley, et al. *The American Tradition in Literature.* Vol. 2. New York: W. W. Norton and Co., 1967.
Kay, Arthur Murray. *The Epic Intent and the American Dream: The Westering Theme in Modern American Narrative Poetry.* Unpublished doctoral dissertation. Ann Arbor: University Microfilms, Mic. 61-2660.
O'Neill, Eugene, Jr. "S. V. Benét: 'John Brown's Body.'" *Saturday Review of Literature* 22 (August 6, 1940). 94–95.
Trumbull, John. *The Connecticut Wits.* New York: T. Y. Crowell Co., 1969. This paperback treats some of the most deservedly obscure early attempts to write the great American epic.

Audiovisual Teaching Materials

Records

Beowulf and Chaucer. Includes "Fight with Grendel" and "Banquet Scene," read by Helge Kokeritz. 1 lp. Lexington Records, No. LE-5505.
Paradise Lost. Includes Book One (complete) and Book Four (lines 1–588, 776–903, and 917-end), read by Anthony Quayle. 2 lp's. Caedmon Records, No. TC-2008.
The Rubaiyat of Omar Khayyam and Sohrab and Rustum. Matthew Arnold's narrative poem "Sohrab and Rustum," read by Alfred Drake. 1 lp. Caedmon Records, No. TC-1023.
The Story of Vergil's Aeneid. Readings in Latin and English by Moses Hadas. 1 lp. Folkways Records, No. FL-99973.
The Inferno—Dante. Selections from Cantos I through VIII, translated and read by John Ciardi. Text included. 1 lp. Folkways Records, No. FW-971.

John Brown's Body. Adapted for dramatic reading for four actors
with chorus. 2 lp's. Columbia Masterworks, No. SL-181.

Films

The Odyssey. Three parts: The Structure of the Epic, The Return
of Odysseus, The Central Themes. 80 minutes, 16mm,
sound, color. Encyclopaedia Britannica, 1966.
Search for Ulysses. 53 minutes, 16mm, sound, b/w. Columbia Broad-
casting System, 1966.
El Cid. 181 minutes, 16mm, sound, color. Allied Artists, 1966.